Fanny Kemble

Notes Upon Some of Shakespeare's Plays

Fanny Kemble

Notes Upon Some of Shakespeare's Plays

ISBN/EAN: 9783337055158

Printed in Europe, USA, Canada, Australia, Japan

Cover: Foto ©Thomas Meinert / pixelio.de

More available books at **www.hansebooks.com**

NOTES

UPON SOME OF

SHAKESPEARE'S PLAYS

By FRANCES ANNE KEMBLE

INTRODUCTION

MACBETH   *THE TEMPEST*
HENRY VIII.   *ROMEO & JULIET*

LONDON
RICHARD BENTLEY & SON
Publishers in Ordinary to Her Majesty the Queen
1882

LIST OF CONTENTS

I. INTRODUCTORY—ON THE STAGE 1

II. NOTES ON MACBETH, NO. 1 . 19

III. NOTES ON MACBETH, NO. 2 47

IV. NOTES ON HENRY VIII. . 81

V. NOTES ON THE TEMPEST, NO. 1 . 101

VI. NOTES ON THE TEMPEST, NO. 2 . 129

VII. NOTES ON THE TEMPEST, NO. 3 . . 137

VIII. NOTES ON ROMEO AND JULIET . . 163

ON THE STAGE.

ON THE STAGE.

THINGS dramatic and things theatrical are often confounded together in the minds of English people, who, being for the most part neither the one nor the other, speak and write of them as if they were identical, instead of, as they are, so dissimilar that they are nearly opposite.

That which is dramatic in human nature is the passionate, emotional, humorous element, the simplest portion of our composition, after our mere instincts, to which it is closely allied, and this has no relation whatever, beyond its momentary excitement and gratification, to that which imitates it, and is its theatrical reproduction; the dramatic is the *real*, of which the theatrical is the *false*.

Both nations and individuals in whom the dramatic temperament strongly preponderates are rather remarkable for a certain vivid simplicity of nature, which produces sincerity and vehemence of emotion and expression, but is entirely without the *consciousness* which is never absent from the theatrical element.

Children are always dramatic, but only theatrical when they become aware that they are objects of admiring attention; in which case the assuming and dissembling capacity of *acting* develops itself comically and sadly enough in them.

The Italians, nationally and individually, are dramatic; the French, on the contrary, theatrical; we English of the present day are neither the one nor the other, though our possession of the noblest dramatic literature in the world proves how deeply at one time our national character was imbued with elements which are now so latent as almost to be of doubtful existence; while, on the other hand, our American progeny are, as a nation, devoid of the dramatic element, and have a considerable infusion of that which is theatrical, delighting, like the Athenians of old, in processions, shows, speeches, oratory, demonstrations, celebrations, and declarations, and such displays of public and private sentiment as would be repugnant to English taste and feeling; to which theatrical tendency, and the morbid love of excitement which is akin to it, I attribute the fact that Americans, both nationally and individually, are capable of a certain sympathy with the French character, in which we are wanting.

The combination of the power of representing passion and emotion with that of imagining or conceiving it—that is, of the theatrical talent with the dramatic temperament—is essential to make a good actor; their combination in the highest possible degree alone makes a great one.

There is a specific comprehension of effect and the means of producing it, which, in some persons, is a distinct capacity, and this forms what actors call the study of their profession; and in this, which is the alloy necessary to make theatrical that which is only dramatic, lies the heart of their mystery and the snare of their craft in more ways than one: and this, the actor's *business*, goes sometimes absolutely against the dramatic temperament, which is nevertheless essential to it.

Every day lessens the frequency of this specific combination among ourselves, for the dramatic temperament, always exceptional in England, is becoming daily more so under the various adverse influences of a state of civilisation and society which fosters a genuine dislike to exhibitions of emotion, and a cynical disbelief in the reality of it, both necessarily repressing, first, its expression, and next, its existence. On the other hand, greater intellectual cultivation and a purer and more elevated taste, are unfavourable to the existence of the true theatrical spirit; and English actors of the present day are of the public, by being "nothing if not critical," and are not of their craft, having literally ceased to know "what belongs to a frippery." They have lost for the most part alike the dramatic emotional temperament and the scenic science of mere effect, and our stage is and must be supplied, if supplied at all, by persons less sophisticated and less civilised. The plays brought out and revived at our theatres of late years bear doleful witness to this. We have in them archæology, ethnology, history, geography, botany (even to the curiosity of ascertaining the Danish wild-flowers that Ophelia might twist with her mad straws), and upholstery; everything, in short, but acting, which it seems we cannot have.

When Mrs. Siddons, in her spectacles and mob-cap, read *Macbeth* or *King John*, it was one of the grandest dramatic achievements that could be imagined, with the least possible admixture of the theatrical element; the representation of the *Duke's Motto*, with all its resources of scenic effect, is a striking and interesting theatrical entertainment, with hardly an admixture of that which is truly dramatic.

Garrick was, I suppose, the most perfect actor that our stage has ever produced, equalling in tragedy and comedy the greatest performers of both; but while his dramatic organisation enabled him to represent with exquisite power and pathos the principal characters of Shakespeare's noblest plays, his theatrical taste induced him to garble, desecrate, and disfigure the masterpieces of which he was so fine an interpreter, in order to produce or enhance those peculiar effects which constitute the chief merit and principal attraction of all theatrical exhibitions.

Mrs. Siddons could lay no claim to versatility—it was not in her nature; she was without mobility of mind, countenance, or manner; and her dramatic organisation was in that respect inferior to Garrick's; but out of a family of twenty-eight persons, all of whom made the stage their vocation, she alone pre-eminently combined the qualities requisite to make a great theatrical performer in the highest degree.

Another member of that family—a foreigner by birth, and endowed with the most powerful and vivid dramatic organisation—possessed in so small a degree the faculty of the stage, that the parts which she represented successfully were few in number, and though among them there were some dramatic *creations* of extraordinary originality and beauty, she never rose to the highest rank in her profession, nor could claim in any sense the title of a great theatrical artist.—This was my mother. And I suppose no member of that large histrionic family was endowed to the same degree with the natural dramatic temperament. The truth of her intonation, accent, and emphasis, made her common speech as good as a play to hear, (oh, how much better than some we *do* hear!) and whereas I have seen the Shakespeare of my father, and the Shakespeare and Milton of Mrs. Siddons, with every emphatic word underlined and accentuated, lest they should omit the right inflection in delivering the lines, my mother could no more have needed such notes whereby to speak *true* than she would a candle to have walked by at noonday. She was an incomparable critic; and though the intrepid sincerity of her nature made her strictures sometimes more accurate than acceptable, they were inestimable for the fine tact for truth, which made her instinctively reject in nature and art whatever sinned against it.

I do not know whether I shall be considered competent to pass a judgment on myself in this matter, but I think I am. Inheriting from my father a theatrical descent of two generations and my mother's vivid and versatile organisation, the stage itself, though it became from the force of circumstances my career, was, partly from my nature, and partly from my education, so repugnant to me, that I failed to accomplish any result at all, worthy of my many advantages. I imagine I disappointed alike those who did and those who did not think me endowed with the talent of my family, and incurred, towards the very close of my theatrical career, the severe verdict from one of the masters of the stage of the present day, that I was "ignorant of the first rudiments of my profession."

In my father and mother I have had frequent opportunities of observing in most marked contrast the rapid intuitive perception of the dramatic instinct in an organisation where it preponderated, and the laborious process of logical argument by which the same result, on a given question, was reached by a mind of different constitution (my father's), and reached with much doubt and hesitation, caused by the very application of analytical reasoning. The slow mental process *might* with time have achieved a right result in all such cases; but the dramatic instinct, aided by a fine organisation, was unerring; and this leads me to observe, that there is no reason whatever to expect that fine actors shall be necessarily profound commentators on the parts that they sustain most successfully, but rather the contrary.

I trust I shall not be found wanting in due respect for the greatness that is gone from us, if I say that Mrs. Siddons' analysis of the part of "Lady Macbeth" was to be found *alone* in her representation of it; of the magnificence of which the "essay" she has left upon the character gives not the faintest idea.

If that great actress had possessed the order of mind capable of conceiving and producing a philosophical analysis of any of the wonderful poetical creations which she so wonderfully embodied, she would surely never have been able to embody them as she did. For to whom are all things given? and to whom were ever given, in such abundant measure, consenting and harmonious endowments of mind and body for the peculiar labour of her life?

The dramatic faculty, as I have said, lies in a power of apprehension quicker than the disintegrating process of critical analysis, and when it is powerful, and the organisation fine, as with Mrs. Siddons, perception rather than reflection reaches the aim proposed; and the persons endowed with this specific gift will hardly unite with it the mental qualifications of philosophers and metaphysicians: no better proof of which can be adduced than Mrs. Siddons herself, whose performances were, in the strict sense of the word, excellent, while the two treatises she has left upon the characters of "Queen Constance" and "Lady Macbeth"—two of her finest parts—are feeble and superficial. Kean, who possessed, beyond all actors whom I have seen, tragic inspiration, could very hardly, I should think, have given a satisfactory reason for any one of the great effects which he produced. Of Mdlle. Rachel, whose impersonations fulfilled to me the idea of perfect works of art of their kind, I have heard, from one who knew her well, that her intellectual processes were limited to the consideration of the most purely mechanical part of her vocation; and Pasta, the great lyric tragedian, who, Mrs. Siddons said, was capable of giving her lessons, replied to the observation, "Vous avez dû beaucoup étudier l'antique,"

"Je l'ai beaucoup senti." The reflective and analytical quality has little to do with the complex process of acting, and is alike remote from what is dramatic and what is theatrical.

There is something anomalous in that which we call the dramatic art that has often arrested my attention and exercised my thoughts; the special gift and sole industry of so many of my kindred, and the only labour of my own life, it has been a subject of constant and curious speculation with me, combining as it does elements at once so congenial and so antagonistic to my nature.

Its most original process, that is, the conception of the character to be represented, is a mere reception of the creation of another mind; and its mechanical part, that is, the representation of the character thus apprehended, has no reference to the intrinsic, poetical, or dramatic merit of the original creation, but merely to the accuracy and power of the actor's perception of it; thus the character of "Lady Macbeth" is as majestic, awful, and poetical, whether it be worthily filled by its pre-eminent representative, Mrs. Siddons, or unworthily by the most incompetent of ignorant provincial tragedy queens.

This same dramatic art has neither fixed rules, specific principles, indispensable rudiments, nor fundamental laws; it has no basis in positive science, as music, painting, sculpture, and architecture have; and differs from them all, in that the mere appearance of spontaneity, which is an acknowledged assumption, is its chief merit. And yet—

> This younger of the sister arts,
> Where all their charms combine—

requires in its professors the imagination of the poet, the ear of the musician, the eye of the painter and sculptor, and over and above these, a faculty peculiar to itself, inasmuch as the actor personally fulfils and embodies his conception; his own voice is his cunningly modulated instrument; his own face the canvas whereon he portrays the various expressions of his passsion; his own frame the mould in which he casts the images of beauty and majesty that fill his brain; and whereas the painter and sculptor may select, of all possible attitudes, occupations, and expressions, the most favourable to the beautiful effect they desire to produce and fix, and bid it so remain fixed for ever, the actor must live and move through a temporary existence of poetry and passion, and preserve throughout its duration that ideal grace and dignity, of which the canvas and the marble give but a silent and motionless image. And yet it is an art that requires no study worthy of the name: it creates nothing—it perpetuates nothing; to its professors, whose personal qualifications form half their merit, is justly given the meed of personal admiration, and the reward of contemporaneous popularity is well bestowed on those whose labour consists in exciting momentary emotion. Their most persevering and successful efforts can only benefit, by a passionate pleasure of at most a few years' duration, the play-going public of their own immediate day, and they are fitly recompensed with money and applause, to whom may not justly belong the rapture of creation, the glory of patient and protracted toil, and the love and honour of grateful posterity.

NOTES ON MACBETH.

No. I.

SOME NOTES UPON THE
CHARACTERS IN SHAKESPEARE'S PLAY OF

MACBETH.

No. I.

MACBETH is pre-eminently the Drama of Conscience. It is the most wonderful history of temptation, in its various agency upon the human soul, that is to be found in the universal range of imaginative literature. Viewed in this aspect, the solemn march of the tragedy becomes awful, and its development a personal appeal, of the profoundest nature, to every one who considers it with that serious attention that its excellence as a work of art alone entitles it to command. To every human soul it tells the story of its own experience, rendered indeed more impressive by the sublime poetry in which it is uttered; but it is the truth itself, and not the form in which it is presented, which makes the force of its appeal; and the terrible truth with which the insidious approach of temptation—its imperceptible advances, its gradual progress, its clinging pertinacity, its recurring importunity, its prevailing fascination, its bewildering sophistry, its pitiless tenacity, its imperious tyranny, and its final hideous triumph over the moral sense—is delineated, that makes *Macbeth* the grandest of all poetical lessons, the most powerful of all purely fictitious moralities, the most solemn of all lay sermons drawn from the text of human nature.

In a small pamphlet, written many years ago by Mr. John Kemble, upon the subject of the character of Macbeth, and which now survives as a mere curiosity of literature, he defends with considerable warmth the hero of the play from a charge of cowardice, brought against him either by Malone or Steevens in some of their strictures on the tragedy.

This charge appeared to me singular, as it would never have occurred to me that there could be two opinions upon the subject of the personal prowess of the soldier; who comes before us heralded by the martial title of Bellona's bridegroom, and wearing the garland of a double victory. But, in treating his view of the question, Mr. Kemble dwells, with extreme and just admiration, upon the skill with which Shakespeare has thrown all the other characters into a shadowy background, in order to bring out with redoubled brilliancy the form of Macbeth when it is first presented to us. Banquo, his fellow in fight and coadjutor in conquest, shares both the dangers and rewards of his expedition; and yet it is the figure of Macbeth which stands out prominently in the van of the battle so finely described by Rosse—it is he whom the king selects as heir to the dignities of the treacherous Thane of Cawdor—it is to meet him that the withered ambassadresses of the powers of darkness float through the lurid twilight of the battle day; and when the throb of the distant drum is heard across the blasted heath, among the host whose tread it times over the gloomy expanse, the approach of one man alone is greeted by the infernal ministers. Their appointed prey draws near, and, with the presentiment of their dire victory over the victor, they exclaim, "A drum! a drum! Macbeth doth come!"

Marshalled with triumphant strains of warlike melody; paged at the heels by his victorious soldiers; surrounded by their brave and noble leaders, himself the leader of them all; flushed with success and crowned with triumph —Macbeth stands before us; and the shaggy brown heath seems illuminated around him with the keen glitter of arms, the waving of bright banners, and broad tartan folds, and the light that emanates from, and surrounds as with a dazzling halo, the face and form of a heroic man in the hour of his success.

Wonderful indeed, in execution as in conception, is this brilliant image of warlike glory! But how much more wonderful, in conception as in execution, is that representation of moral power which Shakespeare has placed beside it in the character of Banquo! Masterly as is the splendour shed around, and by, the prominent figure on the canvas, the solemn grace and dignity of the one standing in the shadow behind it is more remarkable still. How with almost the first words that he speaks the majesty of right asserts itself over that of might, and the serene power of a steadfast soul sheds forth a radiance which eclipses the glare of mere martial glory, as the clear moonlight spreads itself above and beyond the flaring of ten thousand torches.

When the unearthly forms and greeting of the witches have arrested the attention of the warriors, and to the amazement excited in both of them is added, in the breast of one, the first shuddering thrill of a guilty thought which betrays itself in the start with which he receives prophecies which to the ear of Banquo seem only as "things that do sound so fair;" Macbeth has already accepted the first inspiration of guilt—the evil within his heart has quickened and stirred at the greeting of the visible agents of evil, and he is already sin-struck and terror-struck at their first utterance; but like a radiant shield, such as we read of in old magic stories, of virtue to protect its bearer from the devil's assault, the clear integrity of Banquo's soul remains unsullied by the serpent's breath, and, while accepting all the wonder of the encounter, he feels none of the dismay which shakes the spirit of Macbeth—

> "Good sir, why do you start, and seem to fear
> Things that do sound so fair?"

The fair sound has conveyed no foul sense to his perception, but, incited rather by the fear and bewilderment of his usually dauntless companion than by any misgiving of his own (which indeed his calm and measured adjuration shows him to be free from), he turns to these mysterious oracles, and, with that authority before which the devils of old trembled and dispossessed themselves of their prey, he questions, and they reply. Mark the power—

higher than any, save that of God, from which it directly emanates—of the intrepid utterance of an upright human soul—

"In the name of *Truth*, are ye fantastical?"

At that solemn appeal, does one not see hell's agents start and cower like the foul toad touched by the celestial spear? How pales the glitter of the hero of the battle-field before the steadfast shining of this honest man, when to his sacred summons the subject ministers of hell reply true oracles, though uttered by lying lips—sincere homage, such as was rendered on the fields of Palestine by the defeated powers of darkness, to the divine virtue that overthrew them—such as for ever unwilling evil pays to the good which predominates over it, the everlasting subjection of hell to heaven.

"Hail, hail, hail!—lesser than Macbeth, but greater," etc.

And now the confused and troubled workings of Macbeth's mind pour themselves forth in rapid questions, urging one upon another the evident obstacles which crowd, faster than his eager thought can beat them aside, between him and the bait held forth to his ambitious desires; but to *his* challenge, made, not in the name or spirit of truth, but at the suggestion of the grasping devil which is fast growing into entire possession of his heart, no answer is vouchsafed; the witches vanish, leaving the words of impotent and passionate command to fall upon the empty air. The reply to his vehement questioning has already been made; he has *seen*, at one glimpse, in the very darkest depths of his imagination, *how* the things foretold *may* be, and to that fatal answer alone is he left by the silence of those whose mission to him is thenceforth fully accomplished. Twice does he endeavour to draw from Banquo some comment other than that of mere astonishment upon the fortunes thus foretold them :—

> "Your children shall be kings?
> You shall be king?
> And Thane of Cawdor too—went it not so?
> To the self-same tune and words?"

But the careless answers of Banquo unconsciously evade the snare; and it is not until the arrival of Rosse, and his ceremonious greeting of Macbeth by his new dignity of Thane of Cawdor, that Banquo's exclamation of—

"What! can the devil speak true?"

proves at once that he had hitherto attached no importance to the prophecy of the witches, and that, now that its partial fulfilment compelled him to do so, he unhesitatingly pronounces the agency through which their foreknowledge had reached them to be evil. Most significant indeed is the direct, rapid, unhesitating intuition by which the one mind instantly repels the approach of evil, pronouncing it at once to be so, compared with the troubled, perplexed, imperfect process, half mental, half moral, by which the other labours to strangle within himself the pleadings of his better angel:—

" This supernatural soliciting cannot be ill—
Cannot be good! If ill,
Why hath it given me earnest of success
Beginning in a truth? I *am* Thane of Cawdor."

The devil's own logic: the inference of

right drawn from the successful issue, the seal whose stamp, whether false or genuine, still satisfies the world of the validity of every deed to which it is appended. Wiser than all the wisdom that ever was elaborated by human intellect, brighter than any light that ever yet was obtained by process of human thought, juster and more unerringly infallible than any scientific deduction ever produced by the acutest human logic, is the simple instinct of good and evil in the soul that loves the one and hates the other. Like those fine perceptions by which certain delicate and powerful organisations detect with amazing accuracy the hidden proximity of certain sympathetic or antipathetic existences, so the moral sensibility of the true soul recoils at once from the antagonistic principles which it detects with electric rapidity and certainty, leaving the intellect to toil after and discover, discriminate and describe, the cause of the unutterable instantaneous revulsion.

Having now not only determined the nature of the visitation they have received, but become observant of the absorbed and distracted demeanour and countenance of Macbeth, for which he at first accounted guilelessly according to his wont, by the mere fact of natural astonishment at the witches' prophecy and its fulfilment, together with the uneasy novelty of his lately acquired dignities—

"Look how our partner's rapt,
New honours come upon him like our new garments,"
etc.

Banquo is called upon by Macbeth directly for some expression of his own opinion of these mysterious events, and the impression they have made on his mind.

"Do you not hope your children *shall* be kings," etc.

He answers with that solemn warning, almost approaching to a rebuke of the evil suggestion that he now for the first time perceives invading his companion's mind :—

"That trusted home
Might yet enkindle you unto the crown," etc.

It is not a little remarkable that, having in the first instance expressed so strongly his surprise at finding a truth among the progeny of the father of lies, and uttered that fine instinctive exclamation, "What! can the devil speak true?" Banquo, in the final deliberate expression of his opinion to Macbeth upon the subject of the witches' prophecy, warns him against the semblance of truth, that combined with his own treacherous infirmity, is strengthening the temptation by which his whole soul is being searched:—

> "But it is strange,
> And oftentimes to win us to our harm
> The instruments of darkness tell us truths," etc.

Although these two passages may appear at first to involve a contradiction almost, it seems to me that both the sentiments—the brave, sudden denial of any kindred between the devil and truth, and the subsequent admission of the awful mystery by which truth sometimes is permitted to be a two-edged weapon in the armoury of hell—are eminently characteristic of the same mind. Obliged to confess that the devil does speak true sometimes, Banquo, nevertheless, can only admit that he does so for an evil purpose, and this passage is one of innumerable proofs of the general coherence, in spite of apparent discrepancy, in Shakespeare's delineations of character. The same soul of the one man may, with no inconsistency but what is perfectly compatible with spiritual harmony, utter both the sentiments: the one on impulse, the other on reflection.

Here, for the first time, Macbeth encounters the barrier of that uncompromising spirit, that sovereignty of nature, which as he afterwards himself acknowledges "would be feared," and which he does fear and hate accordingly, more and more savagely and bitterly, till detestation of him as his natural superior, terror of him as the possible avenger of blood, and envy of him as the future father of a line of kings, fill up the measure of his murderous ill-will, and thrust him upon the determination of Banquo's assassination; and when, in the midst of his royal banquet-hall, filled with hollow-hearted feasting and ominous revelry and splendour, his conscience conjures up the hideous image of the missing guest, whose health he invokes with lips white with terror, while he knows that his gashed and mangled corpse is lying stark under the midnight rain; surely it is again with this solemn warning, uttered in vain to stay his soul from the perdition yawning for it in the first hour of their joint temptation,—

> "That trusted home
> Might yet enkindle you unto the crown," etc.

that the dead lips appear to move, and the dead eyes are sadly fixed on him, and the heavy locks, dripping with gore, are shaken in silent intolerable rebuke.

In the meeting with the kind-hearted old king, the loyal professions of the two generals are, as might be expected, precisely in inverse ratio to their sincere devotion to Duncan. Banquo answers in a few simple words the affectionate demonstration of his sovereign, while Macbeth, with his whole mind churning round and round like some black whirlpool the murderous but yet unformed designs which have taken possession of it, utters his hollow professions of attachment in terms of infinitely greater warmth and devotion. On the nomination of the king's eldest son to the dignity of Prince of Cumberland, the bloody task which he had already proposed to himself is in an instant doubled on his hands; and instantly, without any of his late misgivings, he deals in imagination with the second human life that intercepts his direct attainment of the crown. This short soliloquy of his ends with some lines which are not more remarkable for the power with which they exhibit the confused and dark heavings of his stormy thoughts than for being the first of three similar adjurations, of various expression, but almost equal poetic beauty :—

> "Stars, hide your fires!
> Let not light see my black and deep desires!
> The eye wink at the hand, yet let that be
> Which the eye fears, when it is done, to see!"

In the very next scene, we have the invocation to darkness with which Lady Macbeth closes her terrible dedication of herself to its ruling powers :—

> "Come, thick night,
> And pall thee in the dunnest smoke of hell," etc.

What can be finer than this peculiar use of the word *pall;* suggestive not only of blackness, but of that funereal blackness in which death is folded up; an image conveying at once absence of light and of life ?—

> "That my keen knife see not the wound it makes,
> Nor heaven peep through the blanket of the dark,
> To cry, Hold! hold!" etc.

The third of these murderous adjurations to the powers of nature for their complicity is uttered by Macbeth in the scene preceding the banquet, when, having contrived the mode of Banquo's death, he apostrophises the approaching night thus :—

> "Come, sealing night!
> Scarf up the tender eye of pitiful day," etc.

(what an exquisite grace and beauty there is in this wonderful line!)

"And with thy bloody and invisible hand
Cancel, and tear to pieces, that great bond,
Which keeps me pale!"

Who but Shakespeare would thus have multiplied expressions of the very same idea with such wonderful variety of power and beauty in each of them?—images at once so similar in their general character, and so exquisitely different in their particular form. This last quoted passage precedes lines which appear to me incomparable in harmony of sound and in the perfect beauty of their imagery: lines on which the tongue dwells, which linger on the ear with a charm enhanced by the dark horror of the speaker's purpose in uttering them, and which remind one of the fatal fascination of the Gorgon's beauty, as it lies in its frame of writhing reptiles, terrible and lovely at once to the beholder:—

"Light thickens, and the crow
Makes wing to the rooky wood."

We see the violet-coloured sky, we feel the soft intermitting wind of evening, we hear the solemn lullaby of the dark fir-forest; the homeward flight of the bird suggests the sweetest images of rest and peace; and, coupled and contrasting with the gradual falling of the dim veil of twilight over the placid face of nature, the remote horror "of the deed of fearful note" about to desecrate the solemn repose of the approaching night, gives to these harmonious and lovely lines a wonderful effect of mingled beauty and terror. The combination of vowels in this line will not escape the ear of a nice observer of the melody of our language: the "rooky wood" is a specimen of a happiness of a sound not so frequent perhaps in Shakespeare as in Milton, who was a greater master of the melody of words.

To return to Banquo: in the scene where he and Macbeth are received with such overflowing demonstrations of gratitude by Duncan, we have already observed he speaks but little; only once indeed, when in answer to the king's exclamation,

"Let me unfold thee, and hold thee to my heart,"

he simply replies—

"There if I grow, the harvest is your own."

But while Macbeth is rapidly revolving in his mind the new difficulties thrown in the way of his ambition, and devising new crimes to overleap lest he fall down upon them, we are left to imagine Banquo as dilating upon his achievements to the king, and finding in his praise the eloquence that had failed him in the professions of his own honest loyalty; for no sooner had Macbeth departed to announce the king's approach to his wife, than Duncan answers to the words spoken aside to him by Banquo:—

"True, worthy Banquo, he *is* full so valiant,
And in his praises I am fed."

This slight indication of the generous disposition that usually lives in holy alliance with integrity and truth is a specimen of that infinite virtue which pervades all Shakespeare's works, the effect of which is felt in the moral harmony of the whole, even by those who overlook the wonderful details by which the general result is produced. Most fitting is it, too, that Banquo should speak the delicious lines by which the pleasant seat of Macbeth's castle is brought so vividly to our senses. The man of temperate passions and calm mind is the devout observer of nature; and thus it is that, in the grave soldier's mouth, the notice of the habits of the guest of summer, "the temple-haunting martlet," is an appropriate beauty of profound significance. Here again are lines whose intrinsic exquisiteness is keenly enhanced by the impending doom which hovers over the kind old king. With a heart overflowing with joy for the success of his arms, and gratitude towards his victorious generals, Duncan stands inhaling the serene summer air, receiving none but sensations of the most pleasurable exhilaration on the threshold of his slaughter-house. The sunny breezy eminence before the hospitable castle gate of his devoted kinsman and subject betrays no glimpse to his delighted spirits of the glimmering midnight chamber, where, between his drunken grooms and his devil-driven assassin, with none to hear his stifled cries for help but the female fiend who listens by the darkened door, his life-blood is to ooze away before the daylight again strikes at the portal by which he now stands rejoicing in the ruddy glow of its departure. Banquo next meets us, as the dark climax is just at hand; the heavens, obedient to the invocation of guilt, have shut their eyes, unwilling to behold the perpetration of the crime about to be committed. The good old king has retired to rest in unusual satisfaction, his host and hostess have made their last lying demonstrations, and are gone to the secret councils of the chamber where they lie in wait. Banquo, unwilling to yield himself to the sleep which treacherously presents to his mind, through the disturbed agency of dreams, the temptation so sternly repelled by his waking thoughts, is about to withdraw, supposing himself the last of all who wake in the castle; for on meeting Macbeth he expresses astonishment that he is not yet abed. How beautiful is the prayer with which he fortifies himself against the nightly visitation of his soul's enemy!—

"Merciful powers,
Restrain in me the accursed thoughts that nature
Gives way to in repose."

Further on the explanation of these lines is found in the brief conversation that follows between himself and Macbeth when he says: "I dreamed last night of the three weird sisters;" and it is against a similar visitation of the powers of darkness during his helpless hours of slumber that he prays to be defended before surrendering himself to the heavy summons that "lies like lead upon him." It is remarkable that Banquo, though his temptation assails him from without in dreams of the infernal prophetesses, prays to be delivered not from them, but from the "accursed thoughts that *nature* gives way to in repose;" referring, and justly, his danger to the complicity with evil in his own nature—that noble nature of which Macbeth speaks as sovereignly virtuous, but of which the mortal infirmity is thus confessed by him who best knows its treacherous weakness.

Banquo next appears in the midst of the hideous uproar consequent upon Duncan's murder, when the vaulted chambers of the castle ring with Macduff's cries to the dead man's sleeping sons—when every door bursts open as with the sweeping of a whirlwind, and half-naked forms, and faces white with sudden terror, lean from every gallery overlooking the great hall, into which pour, like the in-rushing ridges of the tide, the scared and staring denizens of the upper chambers; while along remote corridors echoes the sound of hurrying feet, and inarticulate cries of terror are prolonged through dismal distant passages, and the flare of sudden torches flashes above and below, making the intermediate darkness blacker; and the great stone fortress seems to reel from base to battlement with the horror that has seized like a frenzy on all its inmates. From the midst of this appalling tumult rises the calm voice of the man who remembers that he "stands in the great hand of God," and thence confronts the furious elements of human passion surging and swaying before him.

Banquo stands in the hall of Macbeth's castle, in that sudden surprise of dreadful circumstances alone master of his soul, alone able to appeal to the All-seeing Judge of human events, alone able to advise the actions and guide the counsels of the passion-shaken men around him—a wonderful image of steadfastness in that tremendous chaos of universal dismay and doubt and terror.

This is the last individual and characteristic manifestation of the man. The inevitable conviction of Macbeth's crime, and equally inevitable conviction of the probable truth of the promised royalty of his own children, are the only two important utterances of his that succeed, and these are followed so immediately by his own death that the regretful condemnation of the guilty man, once the object of his affectionate admiration, cannot assume the bitterer character of personal detestation, or the reluctant admission of the truth of the infernal prophecy beguile him into dangerous speculations as to the manner of its fulfilment. The noble integrity of the character is unimpaired to the last.

NOTES ON MACBETH.
No. II.

NOTES ON MACBETH.

No. II.

IN a momentary absence of memory, a friend of mine once suggested to me the idea that Lady Macbeth's exclamation in the sleeping scene—" The Thane of Fife had a wife; where is she now ? "—was a conscience-stricken reference to herself, and her own lost condition. Of course, the hypothesis was immediately abandoned on the recollection that Macbeth never had been Thane of Fife, and that it is Macduff's slaughtered mate Lady Macbeth is dreaming of,—the poor dame who, with all her pretty chickens, was destroyed at one fell swoop by Macbeth's murderous cruelty.

The conversation that ensued led me to reflect on this mistaken suggestion of my friend as involving a much deeper mistake—an important psychological error. Not only the fact was not as suggested, but a fact of that nature, —viz. an accusing return upon herself by Lady Macbeth—could not be. Lady Macbeth, even in her sleep, has no qualms of conscience; her remorse takes none of the tenderer forms akin to repentance, nor the weaker ones allied to fear, from the pursuit of which the tortured soul, seeking where to hide itself, not seldom escapes into the boundless wilderness of madness.

A very able article, published some years ago in the *National Review*, on the character of Lady Macbeth, insists much upon an opinion that she died of remorse, as some palliation of her crimes, and mitigation of our detestation of them. That she died of *wickedness* would be, I think, a juster verdict. Remorse is consciousness of guilt,—often, indeed, no more akin to saving contrition than the faith of devils, who tremble and believe, is to saving faith,— but still consciousness of guilt: and that I think Lady Macbeth never had; though the *unrecognised* pressure of her great guilt killed her. I think her life was destroyed by sin as by a disease of which she was unconscious, and that she died of a broken heart, while the impenetrable resolution of her will remained unbowed. The spirit was willing, but the flesh was weak; the body can sin but so much, and survive; and other deadly passions besides those of violence and sensuality can wear away its fine tissues, and undermine its wonderful fabric. The woman's mortal frame succumbed to the tremendous weight of sin and suffering which her immortal soul had power to sustain; and, having destroyed its temporal house of earthly sojourn, that soul, unexhausted by its wickedness, went forth into its new abode of eternity.

The nature of Lady Macbeth, even when prostrated in sleep before the Supreme Avenger, whom she keeps at bay during her conscious hours by the exercise of her indomitable will and resolute power of purpose, is incapable of any salutary spasm of moral anguish, or hopeful paroxysm of mental horror. The irreparable is still to her the *un*deplorable—" What's done cannot be undone :"—and her slumbering eyes see no more ghosts than her watchful waking ones believe in : " I tell you yet again, Banquo is buried ; he cannot come out of his grave." Never, even in her dreams, does any gracious sorrow smite from her stony heart the blessed brine of tears that wash away sin ; never, even in her dreams, do the avenging furies lash her through purgatorial flames that burn away guilt; and the dreary but undismayed desolation in which her spirit abides for ever, is quite other than that darkness, however deep, which the soul acknowledges, and whence it may yet behold the breaking of a dawn shining far off from round the mercy-seat.

The nightmare of a butcher (could a butcher deserve to be so visited for the unhappy necessity of his calling) is more akin to the hauntings which beset the woman who has strangled conscience and all her brood of pleading angels, and deliberately armed her heart and mind against all those suggestions of beauty or fear which succour the vacillating sense of right in the human soul with promptings less imperative than those of conscience, but of fine subtle power sometimes to supplement her law. Justly is she haunted by "blood," who, in the hour of her atrocities, exclaims to her partner, when his appalled imagination reddens the whole ocean with the bloody hand he seeks to cleanse, "A little water clears us of this deed!" Therefore, blood — the feeling of blood, the sight of blood, the smell of blood — is the one ignoble hideous retribution which has dominion over her. Intruding a moral element of which she is conscious into Lady Macbeth's punishment is a capital error, because her punishment, in its very essence, consists in her infinite distance from all such influences. Macbeth, to the very end, may weep and wring his hands, and tear his hair and gnash his teeth, and bewail the lost estate of his soul, though with him too the dreadful process is one of gradual induration. For he retains the unutterable consciousness of a soul; he has a perception of having sinned, of being fallen, of having wandered, of being lost; and so he cries to his physician for a remedy for that "wounded spirit," heavier to bear than all other conceivable sorrow; and utters, in words bitterer than death, the doom of his own deserted, despised, dreaded, and detested old age. He may be visited to the end by those noble pangs which bear witness to the pre-eminent nobility of the nature he has desecrated, and suggest a re-ascension, even from the bottom of that dread abyss into which he has fallen, but from the depths of which he yet beholds the everlasting light which gives him consciousness of its darkness. But *she* may none of this: she may but feel and see and smell blood; and wonder at the unquenched stream that she still wades in—"Who would have thought the old man to have had so much blood in him?"—and fly, hunted through the nights by that "knocking at the door," which beats the wearied life at last out of her stony heart and seared, impenetrable brain.

I once read a pamphlet that made a very strong impression upon me, on the subject of the possible annihilation of the human soul as the consequence of sin. The author, supposing goodness to be nearness to God, and this to be the cause of vitality in the soul, suggested the idea of a gradual, voluntary departure from God, which should cause the gradual darkening and final utter extinction of the spirit. I confess that this theory of spiritual self-extinction through sin seemed to me a thousand times more appalling than the most terrific vision of everlasting torment.

Taking the view I do of Lady Macbeth's character, I cannot accept the idea (held, I believe, by her great representative, Mrs. Siddons) that in the banquet scene the ghost of Banquo, which appears to Macbeth, is seen at the same time by his wife, but that, in consequence of her greater command over herself, she not only exhibits no sign of perceiving the apparition, but can, with its hideous form and gesture within a few feet of her, rail at Macbeth in that language of scathing irony which, combined with his own terror, elicits from him the incoherent, and yet too dangerously significant appeals with which he agonises her and amazes the court.

To this supposition I must again object that Lady Macbeth is no ghost-seer. She is not of the temperament that admits of such impressions; she is incapable of supernatural terror in proportion as she is incapable of spiritual influences; devils do not visibly tempt, nor angels visibly minister to her; and, moreover, I hold that, as to have seen Banquo's ghost at the banqueting-table would have been contrary to *her* nature, to have done so and persisted in her fierce mocking of her husband's terror, would have been impossible to human nature. The hypothesis makes Lady Macbeth a monster, and there is no such thing in all Shakespeare's plays. That she is godless, and ruthless in the pursuit of the objects of her ambition, does not make her such. Many men have been so; and she is that unusual and unamiable (but not altogether unnatural) creature, a masculine woman, in the only real significance of that much misapplied epithet.

Lady Macbeth was this; she possessed the qualities which generally characterise men, and not women—energy, decision, daring, unscrupulousness; a deficiency of imagination, a great preponderance of the positive and practical mental elements; a powerful and rapid appreciation of what each exigency of circumstance demanded, and the coolness and resolution necessary for its immediate execution. Lady Macbeth's character has more of the essentially manly nature in it than that of Macbeth. The absence of imagination, together with a certain obtuseness of the nervous system, is the condition that goes to produce that rare quality —physical courage—which she possessed in a pre-eminent degree. This combination of deficiencies is seldom found in men, infinitely seldomer in women : and its invariable result is insensibility to many things—among others, insensibility to danger. Lady Macbeth was not so bloody as her husband, for she was by no means equally liable to fear; she would not have hesitated a moment to commit any crime that she considered necessary for her purposes, but she would always have known what were and what were not necessary crimes. We find it difficult to imagine that, if *she* had undertaken the murder of Banquo and Fleance, the latter would have been allowed to escape, and impossible to conceive that she would have ordered the useless and impolitic slaughter of Macduff's family and followers, after he had fled to England, from a mere rabid movement of impotent hatred and apprehension. She was never made savage by remorse, or cruel by terror.

There is nothing that seems to me more false than the common estimate of cruelty, as connected with the details of crime. Could the annals and statistics of murder be made to show the prevailing temper under which the most atrocious crimes have been committed, there is little doubt that those which present the most revolting circumstances of cruelty would be found to have been perpetrated by men of more, rather than less, nervous sensibility, or irritability, than the average; for it is precisely in such organisations that hatred, horror, fear, remorse, dismay, and a certain blind bloodthirsty rage, combine under evil excitement to produce that species of delirium under the influence of which, as of some infernal ecstasy, the most horrible atrocities are perpetrated.

Lady Macbeth was of far too powerful an organisation to be liable to the frenzy of mingled emotions by which her wretched husband is assailed; and when, in the very first hour of her miserable exaltation, she perceives that the ashes of the Dead Sea are to be henceforth her daily bread, when the crown is placed upon her brow, and she feels that the "golden round" is lined with red-hot iron, she accepts the dismal truth with one glance of steady recognition :—

> "Like some bold seer in a trance,
> Beholding all her own mischance,
> Mute—with a glassy countenance."

She looks down the dreary vista of the coming years, and, having admitted that "naught's had, all's spent," dismisses her fate, without further comment, from consideration, and applies herself forthwith to encourage, cheer, and succour, with the support of her superior strength, the finer yet feebler spirit of her husband.

In denying to Lady Macbeth all the peculiar sensibilities of her sex (for they are all included in its pre-eminent characteristic—the maternal instinct—and there is no doubt that the illustration of the quality of her resolution by the assertion that she would have dashed her baby's brains out, if she had sworn to do it, is no mere figure of speech, but very certain earnest) Shakespeare has not divested her of natural feeling to the degree of placing her without the pale of our common humanity. Her husband shrank from the idea of her bearing *women* like herself, but not "males," of whom he thought her a fit mother; and she retains enough of the nature of mankind, if not of womankind, to bring her within the circle of our toleration, and make us accept her as *possible*. Thus the solitary positive instance of her sensibility has nothing especially feminine about it. Her momentary relenting in the act of stabbing Duncan, because he resembled her father as he slept, is a touch of human tenderness by which most men might be overcome, while the smearing her hands in the warm gore of the slaughtered old man is an act of physical insensibility which not one woman out of a thousand would have had nerve or stomach for.

That Shakespeare never imagined Banquo's ghost to be visible to Lady Macbeth in the banquet-hall seems to me abundantly proved (however inferentially) by the mode in which he has represented such apparitions as affecting all the men who in his dramas are subjected to this supreme test of courage,—good men, whose minds are undisturbed by remorse; brave men, soldiers, prepared to face danger in every shape ("but that") in which they may be called upon to meet it. For instance, take the demeanour of Horatio, Marcellus, and Bernardo, throughout the scene so finely expressive of their terror and dismay at the appearance of the ghost, and in which the climax is their precipitating themselves together towards the object of their horror, striking at it with their partisans; a wonderful representation of the effect of fear upon creatures of a naturally courageous constitution, which Shakespeare has reproduced in the ecstasy of terror with which Macbeth himself finally rushes upon the terrible vision which unmans him, and drives it from before him with frantic outcries and despairing gestures.

It is no infrequent exhibition of fear in a courageous boy to fly at and strike the object of his dismay—a sort of instinctive method of ascertaining its nature, and so disarming its terrors; and these men are represented by Shakespeare as thus expressing the utmost impulse of a fear, to the intensity of which their words bear ample witness. Horatio says: "It harrows me with fear and wonder." Bernardo says to him: "How now, Horatio! you tremble and turn pale!" and Horatio, describing the vision and its effect upon himself and his companions, says to Hamlet—

> "Thrice he walk'd
> By their oppress'd and fear-surprised eyes
> Within his truncheon's length, whilst they, *distill'd
> Almost to jelly with the act of fear*," etc.

And it must be remembered that nothing in itself hideous or revolting appeared to these men—nothing but the image of the dead King of Denmark, familiar to them in the majestic sweetness of its countenance and bearing, and courteous and friendly in its gestures; and yet it fills them with unutterable terror. When the same vision appears to Hamlet—a young man with the noble spirit of a prince, a conscience void of all offence, and a heart yearning with aching tenderness towards the father whose beloved image stands before him precisely as his eyes had looked upon and loved it in life—how does he accost it?—

> "What may this mean?
> That thou, *dead corse*, again in complete steel,
> Revisit'st thus the glimpses of the moon,
> *Making night hideous*, and we fools of nature
> *So horribly to shake our dispositions*," etc.

The second time that Hamlet sees his father's ghost, when one might suppose that something of the horror attendant upon such a visitation would have been dispelled by the previous experience, his mother thus depicts the appearance that he presents to her—

> "Forth at your eyes your spirits wildly peep;
> And, as the sleeping soldiers in the alarm,
> Your bedded hair, like life in excrements,
> Starts up and stands on end."

What a description of the mere physical revulsion with which living flesh and blood shrinks from the cold simulacrum of life—so like and so utterly unlike—so familiar and yet so horribly strange! The agony is physical—not of the soul; for

> "What can it do to that,
> Being a thing immortal as itself?"

exclaims the undaunted spirit of the young

man; and in the closet scene with his mother passionate pity and tenderness for his father are the only emotions Hamlet expresses with his lips, while his eyes start from their sockets, and his hair rears itself on his scalp, with the terror inspired by the proximity of that "gracious figure."

In "Julius Cæsar," the emotion experienced by Brutus at the sight of Cæsar's ghost is, if possible, even more to the purpose. The spirit of the firm Roman, composed to peaceful meditation after his tender and sweet reconciliation with his friend, and his exquisite kindness to his sleepy young slave, is quietly directed to the subject of his study, when the ghost of Cæsar appears to him, darkening by its presence the light of the taper by which he reads, and to which Shakespeare, according to the superstition of his day, imparts this sensitiveness to the preternatural influence. Brutus, in questioning his awful visitor, loses none of his stoical steadfastness of soul, and yet speaks of his blood running cold, and his hair *staring* with the horror of the unearthly visitation.

Surely, having thus depicted the effect of such an experience on such men as Horatio, Hamlet, Brutus, and Macbeth, Shakespeare can never have represented a woman, even though that woman was the bravest of her sex, and almost of her kind, as subjected to a like ordeal and utterly unmoved by it. An argument which appears to me conclusive on the point however, is, that in the sleeping scene Lady Macbeth divulges nothing of the kind; and, even if it were possible to conceive her intrepidity equal to absolute silence and self-command under the intense and mingled terrors of the banquet scene *with* a perception of Banquo's apparition, it is altogether impossible to imagine that the emotion she controlled then should not reveal itself in the hour of those unconscious confessions when she involuntarily strips bare the festering plagues of her bosom to the night, and to her appalled watchers, and in her ghastly slumbers, with the step and voice of some horrible automaton, moved by no human volition, but a dire lash and goad him past the obstruction of his own terrors, her habitual tone, from beginning to end, is of a sort of contemptuous compassion towards the husband whose moral superiority of nature she perceives and despises, as men not seldom put by the finer and truer view of duty of women, as too delicate for common use, a weapon of too fine a temper for worldly warfare.

Her analysis of his character while still holding in her hand his affectionate letter, her admonition to him that his face betrays the secret disturbance of his mind, her advice that he will commit the business of the King's murder to her management, her grave and almost kind solicitude at his moody solitary brooding over the irretrievable past, and her compassionate suggestion at the close of the banquet scene,—

"You want the season of all natures—sleep,"

when she must have seen the utter hopelessness of long concealing crimes which the miserable murderer would himself inevitably reveal in some convulsion of ungovernable remorse, are all indications of her own sense of superior power over the man whose nature wants the "illness" with which hers is so terribly endowed, who would "holily" that which he would "highly," who would not "play false," and yet would "wrongly win."

Nothing, indeed, can be more wonderfully perfect than Shakespeare's delineation of the evil nature of these two human souls—the evil strength of the one, and the evil weakness of the other.

The woman's wide-eyed, bold, collected leap into the abyss makes us gulp with terror; while we watch the man's blinking, shrinking, clinging, gradual slide into it, with a protracted agony akin to his own.

In admirable harmony with the conception of both characters is the absence in the case of Lady Macbeth of all the grotesquely terrible supernatural machinery by which the imagination of Macbeth is assailed and daunted. She reads of her husband's encounter with the witches, and the fulfilment of their first prophecy; and yet, while the men who encounter them (Banquo as much as Macbeth) are struck and fascinated by the wild quaintness of their weird figures,—with the description of which it is evident Macbeth has opened his letter to her,—her mind does not dwell for a moment on these "weak ministers" of the great power of evil. The metaphysical conception of the influence to which she dedicates herself is pure free-thinking compared with the superstitions of her times; and we cannot imagine her sweeping into the murky cavern, where the hellish juggleries of Hecate are played, and her phantasmagories revel round their filthy cauldron, without feeling that these petty devils would shrink appalled away from the presence of the awful woman who had made her bosom the throne of those "murdering ministers" who in their "sightless substance" attend on "nature's mischief."

Nor has Shakespeare failed to show how

well, up to a certain point, the devil serves those who serve him well. The whole-hearted wickedness of Lady Macbeth buys that exemption from "present fears" and "horrible imaginings" which Macbeth's half-allegiance to right cannot purchase for him. In one sense, good consciences—that is, tender ones—may be said to be the only bad ones: the very worst alone are those that hold their peace and cease from clamouring. In sin, as in all other things, thoroughness has its reward; and the reward is blindness to fear, deafness to remorse, hardness to good, and moral insensibility to moral torture—the deadly gangrene instead of the agony of cauterisation; a degradation below shame, fear, and pain. This point Lady Macbeth reaches at once, while from the first scene of the play to the last the wounded soul of Macbeth writhes and cries and groans over its own gradual deterioration. Incessant returns upon himself and his own condition, betray a state of moral disquietude which is as ill-boding an omen of the spiritual state as the morbid feeling of his own pulse by a sickly self-observing invalid is of the physical condition; and, from the beginning to the end of his career, the several stages of his progress in guilt are marked by his own bitter consciousness of it. First, the startled misgiving as to his own motives:

> "This supernatural soliciting
> Cannot be ill—cannot be good."

Then the admission of the necessity for the treacherous cowardly assumption of friendly hospitality, from which the brave man's nature and soldier's alike revolt:

> "False face must hide what the false heart doth know."

Then the panic-stricken horror of the insisting:

> "But *why* could not I pronounce Amen?
> I had most need of blessing, and Amen
> Stuck in my throat."

The vertigo of inevitable retribution:

> "Glamis doth murder sleep,
> And therefore Cawdor shall sleep no more,
> Macbeth shall sleep no more!"

The utter misery of the question:

"How is it with me, when ev'ry noise appals me?"

The intolerable bitterness of the thought :

> "For Banquo's issue have I *filed my breast*,
> And mine *eternal jewel* given ;
> Given to the common enemy of mankind."

Later comes the consciousness of stony loss of fear and pity :

> "The time has been
> My senses would have cool'd to hear a night-shriek.
> . . . .
> Direness, familiar to my slaughterous thoughts,
> Cannot once stir me !"

After this, the dreary wretchedness of his detested and despised old age confronts him :

> "And that which should accompany old age,
> As honour, love, obedience, troops of friends,
> I must not look to have."

Most wonderful of all is it, after reviewing the successive steps of this dire declension of the man's moral nature, to turn back to his first acknowledgment of that Divine government, that Supreme Rule of Right, by which the deeds of men meet righteous retribution. "*Here*, even *here*, upon this bank and shoal of

Time;" that unhesitating confession of faith in the immutable justice and goodness of God with which he first opens the debate in his bosom, and contrasts it with the desperate blasphemy which he utters in the hour of his soul's final overthrow, when he proclaims life—man's life, the precious and mysterious object of God's moral government—

> "A tale told by an idiot, full of sound and fury,
> *Signifying nothing!*"

The preservation of Macbeth's dignity in a degree sufficient to retain our sympathy, in spite of the preponderance of his wife's nature over his, depends on the two facts of his undoubted heroism in his relations with men, and his great tenderness for the woman whose evil will is made powerful over his partly by his affection for her. It is remarkable that hardly one scene passes where they are brought together in which he does not address to her some endearing appellation; and, from his first written words to her whom he calls his "Dearest partner of greatness," to his pathetic appeal to her physician for some alleviation of her moral plagues, a love of extreme strength and tenderness is constantly manifested in every address to or mention of her that he makes. He seeks her sympathy alike in the season of his prosperous fortune and in the hour of his mental anguish:

"Oh, full of scorpions is my mind, dear wife!"

and in this same scene there is a touch of essentially manly reverence for the womanly nature of her who has so little of it, that deserves to be classed among Shakespeare's most exquisite inspirations:—his refusing to pollute his wife's mind with the bloody horror of Banquo's proposed murder.

"Be innocent of the knowledge, dearest chuck!"

is a conception full of the tenderest and deepest refinement, contrasting wonderfully with the hard, unhesitating cruelty of her immediate sugggestion in reply to his:

"Thou know'st that Banquo and his Fleance live,
But in them Nature's copy's not eterne;"

by which she clearly demonstrates that her own wickedness not only keeps pace with his, but has indeed, as in the business of the King's murder, reached at a bound that goal towards which he has struggled by slow degrees.

At the end of the banquet scene he appeals to her for her opinion on the danger threatened by Macduff's contumacious refusal of their invitation, and from first to last he so completely leans on her for support and solace in their miserable partnership of guilt and woe, that when we hear the ominous words:

"My Lord, the Queen is dead!"

we see him stagger under the blow which strikes from him the prop of that undaunted spirit in whose valour he found the never-failing stimulus of his own.

In the final encounter between Macbeth and the appointed avenger of blood it appears to me that the suggestion of his want of personal courage, put forward by some commentators on his character, is most triumphantly refuted.

Until his sword crosses that of Macduff, and the latter, with his terrible defiance to the "*Angel*"[1] whom Macbeth still has served, reveals to him the fact of his untimely birth, he has been like one drunk—maddened by the poisonous inspirations of the hellish oracles in which he has put his faith; and his furious excitement is the delirium of mingled doubt and dread with which he clings, in spite of the gradual revelation of its falsehood, to the juggling promise which pronounced him master of a charmed life. But no sooner is the mist of this delusion swept from his mind, by the piercing blast of Macduff's interpretation of the promise, than the heroic nature of the man once more proclaims itself. The fire of his spirit flames above the "ashes of his chance;" the

---

[1] Noteworthy, in no small degree, is this word "*Angel*" here used by Macduff. Who but Shakespeare would not have written "*Devil*"? But what a tremendous vision of terrible splendour the word evokes! what a visible presence of gloomy glory—even as of the great prince of pride, ambition, and rebellion—seems to rise in lurid majesty, and overshadow the figure of the baffled votary of evil!

intrepid courage of the great chieftain leaps up again in one last blaze of desperate daring; and alone—deserted by his followers and betrayed by his infernal allies—he stands erect in the undaunted bravery of his nature, confronting the eyes of Death as they glare at him from Macduff's sockets, and exclaims, "Yet will I try the last." One feeling only mingles with this expiring flash of resolute heroism, one most pathetic reference to the human detestation from which in that supreme hour he shrinks as much as from degradation—more than from death.

> "I will not yield,
> To kiss the ground before young Malcolm's foot,
> And to be baited by the rabble's curse."

It is the last cry of the human soul, cut off from the love and reverence of humanity; and with that he rushes out of the existence made intolerable by the hatred of his kind.

NOTES ON HENRY VIII.

NOTES ON THE CHARACTERS OF QUEEN
KATHARINE AND CARDINAL WOLSEY
IN SHAKESPEARE'S PLAY OF

HENRY VIII.

THE Queen and Wolsey in Henry VIII. are both types of pride, and yet there is an essential difference in the pride which they each represent. Undoubtedly, the pride of birth and the mere pride of power (whether that power be derived from wealth, intellect, or exaltation of station) are very different things. Katharine represents the pure pride of birth, and Wolsey that of power. Pride of birth, the noblest species of the vice, is not incompatible with considerable personal humility, and the proof that Shakespeare thought so may be found in the Queen's frequently modest and humble mention of herself, her infinite deference to the King, and the repeated reference by the other characters in the play to her meek and quiet spirit. That this pride sometimes consorts with humbleness arises from the fact that it does not rest on any personal, individual quality or achievement, and is therefore less directly egotistical and selfish than the other; and being of a less gross quality is oftener the snare of noble and refined minds, from which, when once possessed by it, it will hardly endure to be eradicated. For it becomes bound up with feelings of personal honour, family honour, and the order and economy of the body social and political, of which nobility forms a principal sustaining pillar in countries whose governments admit it as an integral part of their existence, and in upholding their particular portion of which nobly-born persons, proud of their birth, conceive that they contribute to maintain the whole. Birth, too, with such persons, if they be otherwise virtuously inclined, becomes to them a spur and incitement to high and lofty thoughts and deeds; for how runs the French device, *Noblesse oblige?*—a very weighty and worthy truth, making of high birth a solemn trust to be solemnly fulfilled and answered for. Such, I think, is the pride of some members of the English aristocracy even in these democratic days; such was the family pride of many gentlemen of old and honourable name formerly in England; and, tainted as it is with mortal infirmity, there is but one better thing to be put in its place. The humility of a true Christian is doubtless a grander thing than the gentility of a true gentleman or the nobility of a true nobleman : meantime that man and that nation are in ill case in whom neither is to be found. Of this loftyseeming sin, this pride of birth, Shakespeare's Queen Katharine is a most perfect type, as well as an instance of the (almost) impossibility of a mind once infected with it ever losing the taint. No change of outward circumstance can affect it, and loss of fortune and decline of station can only tend to increase, in those who have it, their veneration for a species of distinction compatible with the narrowest means and lowliest obscurity. The pride of power, that pride which Wolsey exhibits, is, on the contrary, almost invariably arrogant, and very seldom co-exists with any personal humility; for it springs generally from a consciousness of personal merit, strength, capacity, good fortune or achievement, and thus is necessarily grossly egotistical.

Again, the pride of birth is comparatively a relative thing, and has, as it were, a scale or standard by which it is graduated and moderated. The self-respect of those who entertain it naturally involves their respect for those who claim in any degree, whether more or less than themselves, the same distinction, whereas the pride of power is apt to lose all sense of comparison in its overweening self-consciousness: it knows no scale of degree, for its boast is to break down or overleap all such, and its measure is never the claims of others, but its own performed or possible achievement; and it is consequently in perpetual peril of losing all balance. Nobly-born persons invariably speak respectfully of the ancient birth of others: their pride is of a determinate place in a settled system, while the other temper delights in nothing so much as in overturning established order by the self-created precedent of individual ability and success. To this Wolsey's whole language and demeanour during his prosperity bear ample witness: his insolence to the noblemen and gentlemen of the court is nothing more than a species of revenge taken by the butcher's son upon the sons of noblemen and gentlemen for being born such. Those who "achieve greatness" do not always, therefore, encounter with perfect equanimity those who are "born great:" it takes a spirit of rather unusual natural nobility to do so, and the dignity which is not shaken by falling is as nothing to the dignity which is not fluttered by rising. Wolsey, though he had made himself cardinal and hoped to make himself pope, could not unmake himself a butcher's son; and the serene sense of social superiority which men of high and princely birth had over him in this respect galled his consciousness of general power, in which he so greatly excelled them, with a bitter sense of utter impotence in this one particular. To this species of aggressive pride may be attributed the insane arrogance of his "Ego et Rex meus." To the noble Suffolk, the princely Buckingham, or the royal daughter of Spain, Katharine of Aragon, such a form of speech would have seemed nothing short of an audacious act of treason, an offence against order, duty, and majesty, a confounding of those all but sacred social laws by which they themselves were upheld in their several high spheres of state. In the gross-minded, low-born "fellow of Ipswich," whose vigorous intellect and powerful will had raised him to strange heights of glory, it was the mere excess and intoxication of the sense of self-made greatness, which had learned to look upon coronets and crowns, and the papal tiara itself, as the instruments or prizes of its daring ambition, to be used or won, but never respected by him with that religious veneration which men of true nobility have felt for them. To him they were merely the noble means of base self-aggrandisement.

On the other hand, though this species of pride is so much grosser and more vulgar and offensive, I believe it will always be found more easily capable of cure and eradication than the other. The circumstances once altered under which personal power was or could be successfully exercised, consciousness of weakness and defeat almost inevitably ensues; uncertainty, self-distrust, and a sense of insecurity are engendered by failure; a lowered estimate of capacity to achieve things not unnaturally brings with it lessened value of the achievement. For we betake ourselves, as the fox of ancient times has testified ever since his day, to underprize that which is beyond our reach, however much we may have overprized while compassing or possessing it. After this lowering process, and in the vacancy of disappointment, a mortification of spirit sometimes ensues upon which a true humility might possibly engraft itself. Thus, Wolsey might have become humble when once hopelessly fallen from his high fortune, because, ruined, he was nothing in the world's account but the butcher's son, all whose personal ability had not sufficed to retain his great position, and might not suffice to regain it. In this predicament the nobler powers of his mind, shifting their point of view so as to take in more than the mere worldly value of his lost prosperity, might present to him a higher and holier standard by which his estimate of the earthly greatness he had forfeited would become more just, and his wisdom and learning and powerful intellectual faculties, chastened in their action by the sweet uses of adversity, might finally produce in him the grace of meekness and humility. The soil, loosened by the uprooting of the rank and noxious weeds of worldly pride and ambition, and harrowed by the bitterness of worldly failure, might become fit for the good seed and harvest of a wholesome abasement. And in Griffith's account of the great cardinal's death to Queen Katharine he insists upon this very result of his downfall, and the dying man's pathetic words confirm the statement:

> "O father abbot,
> An old man, broken with the storms of state,
> Is come to lay his weary bones among ye:
> Give him a little earth for charity."

The insertion of this historically true appeal in the description of Wolsey's last hours seems to me purely Shakespearian, in spite of the internal evidence upon the strength of which the authorities pronounce these speeches of Griffith's to have been written by Fletcher. Not so Katharine. All the virtue and wisdom she was mistress of could not make her humble, because she was, and remained through ruin and disgrace, even unto "beggarly divorcement" and death, the daughter of the king of Spain, the wife of two kings of England, and felt herself bound, by all the religion and superstition of early training and long habit, to honour her station in herself. So with disgraces *grew* her pride; and with one dying hand stretched out to receive the heavenly crown she was about to put on, with the other she imperiously commanded homage to that earthly one which had been rudely snatched from her brows. Wolsey honoured himself in his station: it was to him the palpable proof of his own great powers of achievement, and when he lost it his confidence in himself must have been shaken to its foundations, and he may almost have fallen into the hopelessness of self-contempt. With what a poisonous bitterness of absolute defeat does he utter the words—

> "O Cromwell,
> The king has gone beyond me: all my glories
> In that one woman I have lost for ever."

Henry VIII. was the favourite play of Dr. Johnson, who does not appear to have entertained the doubts of modern commentators as to its being the work of Shakespeare; and his admiration of it is characteristic when one considers the great wisdom and fine morality by which the whole composition is pervaded. He told Mrs. Siddons that his highest enjoyment would be to see her perform Queen Katharine, for whose character, as delineated by Shakespeare, he had the most unbounded enthusiasm — naturally enough, as it is impossible to conceive a more perfect embodiment of the pure spirit of Toryism. The character is one of great simplicity, and hence in part the impression of grandeur it produces. Instead of the infinitely various motives, feelings, passions, and inclinations which make of most human characters such pieces of involved and complex moral machinery, two strongly developed elements alone compose the woman Shakespeare has copied from Nature and history—a profoundly conscientious and devout spirit, almost saint-like in its obedience to right and duty as she conceived of them, and a towering and indomitable spirit of pride, which so alloyed the more heavenly dispositions as to give harshness and narrowness to a nature otherwise noble, and stamp with its own peculiarly rigid and stern image of royalty the pure gold of her high and virtuous qualities. Every speech Shakespeare puts into her mouth testifies to the wonderful discrimination with which he has delineated this combination of qualities, from her first solemn rebuke to the Duke of Buckingham's surveyor when she bids him beware lest in maligning a noble person he should peril his own nobler soul (her respect for the earthly dignity of the great peer being only outweighed by her respect for an immortal spirit), to the last dying words gasped from the wan and withered lips, when, later even than the desire she expresses that honour may be paid to her as a chaste wife, she commands that honour shall be paid to her as a queen and daughter of a king. This last touching and terrible utterance of the mingled virtue and vice is, as becomes the last, awful and pathetic, though less dramatically striking, perhaps, than the burst of sudden passion when, with her face yet radiant with the reflection of the heavenly vision in which she has received the homage of glorified spirits, with the crown of immortality descending upon her pale, illumined brow, and that "celestial harmony she goes to" resounding in her ears, upon the very threshold of heaven, she turns with such implacable resentment from the poor servant whose "haste had made him unmannerly," and who forgot to approach her kneeling:

> "But this fellow
> Let me ne'er see again."

In her most touching recommendation of her faithful women to the ambassador Capucius she characteristically sums up their praise by saying they will deserve good husbands, even —*noble* men.

But, to me, the most masterly touch of delineation by which Shakespeare has given this moral portrait its greatest perfection is in the Queen's speech on Wolsey's character, when, first of all his sins, she enumerates his "unbounded stomach," that made him "ever rank himself with princes;" and that wonderful line where she says:

> "*I' the presence*
> He would say untruths."

To her, the devout, the upright, the true in spirit, in deed and in word, Wolsey's falsehood was aggravated by its perpetration before Henry VIII., and the sin against God's sovereign majesty of truth assumed a deeper dye in Katharine of Aragon's judgment when committed in the royal presence of the King and Queen of England.

In the great scene with the cardinals Shakespeare has followed Cavendish's *Life of Wolsey* all but verbatim, even to the skein of sewing-materials the good Queen had round her neck. I wonder if his extreme admiration and commendation of Anne Bullen's beauty was justified by the fact, or was only a courtly compliment to her daughter? Holbein's pictures of her do not, I think (even allowing for the ungainly, unbecoming dress), establish her claim to being "the goodliest woman that ever lay by man;"

and then the recollection of her superfluous fingers and toes interferes extremely with whatever other charms she may be supposed to have possessed, though Francis I., who (if all tales be true) admired her very much, was a connoisseur in matters of female beauty. A deficiency in such natural extremities is far less repulsive than an overplus: the one might be the result of accident, the other is pure monstrosity; and all the excellence of that worthiest woman, Katharine, did not prevent her being woman enough to insist upon her fair six-fingered rival perpetually playing at cards in the king's presence. It is amusing to see with what spiteful delight English visitors are shown, among the manuscripts in the Vatican, the original love-letters of Henry VIII. and Anne Bullen. The pope had certainly no special reason to be tender of the honour of either party.

What romantic associations are suggested by the mere reading of the *dramatis personæ* of this play! Brandon, Earl of Suffolk, is here, the lover of Mary Tudor (the king of England's sister, the king of France's wife), the bearer of that charming and chivalrous device, the mingled cloth of frieze and gold:

> "Cloth of gold, do not despise
> That thou art mixed with cloth of frieze:
> Cloth of frieze, be not too bold
> That thou art mixed with cloth of gold."

And Surrey is here, the princely poet, the devoted lover, who, wandering beneath the bright Italian skies, invoked the aid of magic, and conjured up, to cheat his longing senses, the image of his English mistress, the fair Geraldine. How sweet a line there is in the Epilogue to this play when Shakespeare commends the piece to "the merciful construction of good women," even for the sake of the image of one therein most faithfully portrayed!

Upon the whole, however, the play is heavy, and, though replete with fine passages and scenes of great power, fails to awaken or keep alive any intense interest. The recurrence of three scenes, so nearly resembling each other in subject, and even in some degree in treatment, as the death of Buckingham, the downfall of Wolsey, and the death of Katharine, produces a sense of sameness and monotony, though the variety in similarity is very wonderful. The death of Katharine ends the interest of the piece, and the venomous squabbling of the clergymen and the voice of the jubilant throngs, whose acclamations rend the sky at the baptism of the Princess Elizabeth, break harshly on the silence which settles solemnly round the dying Queen in the dim stillness of her deserted sick-chamber at Kimbolton. The noble lines at the conclusion of *Henry VIII.* and the supplementary compliment to James are beyond a doubt to be attributed to Fletcher, with whose manner they are distinctly stamped. To his stately pen may probably also be referred the eulogium on Wolsey spoken by Griffith, and Wolsey's own famous farewell to all his greatness. The passages of the play which are put into *Readers*, and which our schoolboys declaim, are of doubtful authorship perhaps; but who, if not Shakespeare, wrote the scene between the angry king and the ruined cardinal, or that between Wolsey and the lords, or Lady Denny and Anne Bullen's scene on the promotion of the latter to be Marchioness of Pembroke? and who the whole of the King's part, who all the *living* portion of the play, but Shakespeare? Undoubtedly, there were giants in those days in the art of play-writing, but it is by their side that we best measure the stature of him who was taller by the head and shoulders than all the rest, in whose incomparable genius the dramatic intellect of that great mental epoch reached its climax. I have read lately of comparisons between *Henry VIII.* and Tennyson's *Queen Mary:* to me this latter production appears no more like Shakespeare's writing than a suit of his clothes would be like him: they would certainly remind any one who saw them of him who had worn them. I am much mistaken if Alfred Tennyson himself would not be more apt than any one to say (if it may unprofanely be said), "Why callest thou me Shakespeare?"

NOTES ON THE TEMPEST.

No. I.

SOME NOTES ON
THE TEMPEST.

No. I.

IN 1849, the discovery by Mr. Payne Collier of a copy of the Works of Shakespeare, known as the folio of 1632, with manuscript notes and emendations of the same or nearly the same date, created a great and general interest in the world of letters.

The marginal notes were said to be in a handwriting not much later than the period when the volume came from the press; and Shakespearian scholars and students of Shakespeare, and the far more numerous class, lovers of Shakespeare, learned and unlearned, received with respectful eagerness a version of his text claiming a date so near to the lifetime of the master that it was impossible to resist the impression that the alterations came to the world with only less weight of authority than if they had been undoubtedly his own.

The general satisfaction of the literary world in the treasure-trove was but little alloyed by the occasional cautiously-expressed doubts of some caviller at the authenticity of the newly discovered "curiosity of literature;" the daily newspapers made room in their crowded columns for extracts from the volume; the weekly journals put forth more elaborate articles on its history and contents; and the monthly and quarterly reviews bestowed their longer and more careful criticism upon the new readings of that text, to elucidate which has been the devout industry of some of England's ripest scholars and profoundest thinkers; while the actors, not to be behindhand in a study especially concerning their vocation, adopted with more enthusiasm than discrimination some of the new readings, and showed a laudable acquaintance with the improved version, by exchanging undoubtedly the better for the worse, upon the authority of Mr. Collier's folio. Shortly after its publication I had the ill-fortune to hear a popular actress destroy the effect and meaning of one of the most powerful passages in *Macbeth*, by substituting the new for the old reading of the line,—

"What beast was it, then,
That made you break this enterprise to me?"

The cutting antithesis of "What *beast*," in retort to her husband's assertion, "I dare do all that may become a *man*," was tamely rendered by the lady, in obedience to Mr. Collier's folio, "What *boast* was it, then,"—a change that any one possessed of poetical or dramatic perception would have submitted to upon nothing short of the positive demonstration of the author's having so written the passage.

Opinions were, indeed, divided as to the intrinsic merit of the emendations or alterations. Some of the new readings were undoubted improvements, some were unimportant, and others again were beyond all controversy inferior to the established text of the passages; and it seemed not a little difficult to reconcile the critical acumen and poetical insight of many of the corrections with the feebleness and prosaic triviality of others.

Again, it was observed by those conversant with the earlier editions, especially with the little read or valued Oxford edition, that a vast number of the passages given as emendations in Mr. Collier's folio were precisely the same in Hanmer's text. Indeed, it seems not a little remarkable that neither Mr. Collier nor his opponents have thought it worth their while to state that nearly half, and that undoubtedly the better half of the so-called new readings are to be found in the finely printed, but little esteemed, text of the Oxford Shakespeare. If, indeed, these corrections now come to us with the authority of a critic but little removed from Shakespeare's own time, it is remarkable that Sir Thomas Hanmer's, or rather Mr. Theobald's, ingenuity should have forestalled the *fiat* of Mr. Collier's folio in so many instances. On the other hand, it may have been judged by others besides a learned editor of Shakespeare from whom I once heard the remark, that the fact of the so-called new readings being many of them in Rowe and Hanmer, and therefore well known to the subsequent editors of Shakespeare, who nevertheless did not adopt them, proved that in their opinion they were of little value and less authority. But, says Mr. Collier, inasmuch as they are in the folio of 1632, which I now give to the world, they are of authority paramount to any other suggestion or correction that has hitherto been made on the text of Shakespeare.

Thus stood the question in 1853. How stands it a few years later? After a slow, but gradual process of growth and extension of doubt and questionings, more or less calculated to throw discredit on the authority of the marginal notes in the folio,—the volume being subjected to the careful and competent examination of certain officers of the library of the British Museum,— the result seems to threaten a considerable reduction in the supposed value of the authority which the public was called upon to esteem so highly.

The ink in which the annotations are made has been subjected to chemical analysis, and betrays, under the characters traced in it, others made in pencil, which are pronounced by some persons of a more modern date than the letters which have been traced over them.

Here at present the matter rests. Much angry debate has ensued between the various gentlemen interested in the controversy, Mr. Collier not hesitating to suggest that pencil-marks in imitation of his handwriting had been inserted in the volume, and a fly-leaf abstracted from it, while in the custody of Messrs. Hamilton and Madden of the British Museum; while the replies of these gentlemen would go towards establishing that the corrections are forgeries, and insinuating that they are forgeries for which Mr. Collier is himself responsible.

While the question of the antiquity and authority of these marginal notes remains thus undecided, it may not be amiss to apply to them the mere test of common sense in order to determine upon their intrinsic value, to the adequate estimate of which all thoughtful readers of Shakespeare must be to a certain degree competent.

The curious point, of whose they are, may test the science of decipherers of palimpsest manuscripts; the more weighty one, of what they are worth, remains as it was from the first, a matter on which every student of Shakespeare may arrive at some conclusion for himself. And, indeed, to this ground of judgment Mr. Collier himself appeals, in his preface to the "Notes and Emendations," in no less emphatic terms than the following:—
"As Shakespeare was especially the poet of common life, so he was emphatically the poet of common sense; and to the verdict of

common sense I am willing to submit all the more material alterations recommended on the authority before me."

I take "The Tempest," the first play in Mr. Collier's volume of "Notes and Emendations," and, while bestowing my principal attention on the inherent worth of the several new readings, shall point out where they tally exactly with the text of the Oxford edition, because that circumstance has excited little attention in the midst of the other various elements of interest in the controversy, and also because I have it in my power to give from a copy of that edition in my possession some passages corrected by John and Charles Kemble, who brought to the study of the text considerable knowledge of it and no inconsiderable ability for poetical and dramatic criticism.

In the first scene of the first act of "The Tempest," Mr. Collier gives the line,—

"Good Boatswain, have care,"—

adding, "It may be just worth remark, that the colloquial expression is *have a care*, and *a* is inserted in the margin of the corrected folio, 1632, to indicate, probably, that the poet so wrote it, or, at all events, that the actor so delivered it.

In the copy of Hanmer in my possession, the *a* is also inserted in the margin, upon the authority of one of the eminent actors above mentioned.

Scene II.

"The sky, it seems, would pour down stinking pitch,
But that the sea, mounting to the welkin's cheek,
Dashes the fire out."

The manuscript corrector of the folio, 1632, has substituted *heat* for "cheek," which appears to me an alteration of no value whatever. Shakespeare was more likely to have written *cheek* than *heat*; for elsewhere he uses the expression, "Heaven's face," "the welkin's face," and, though irregular, the expression is poetical.

At Miranda's exclamation,—

"A brave vessel,
Who had no doubt some noble creature in her
Dash'd all to pieces,"—

Mr. Collier does Theobald the justice to observe that he, as well as the corrector of the folio, 1632, adds the necessary letter *s* to the word "creature," making the plural substantive agree with her other exclamation of, "Poor souls, they perished!"

Where Mr. Collier, upon the authority of his folio, substitutes *pre*vision for "*pro*vision" in the lines of Prospero,—

> "The direful spectacle of the wreck
> . . . . . .
> I have with such provision in mine art
> So safely ordered," etc.,—

I do not agree to the value of the change. It is very true that *pre*vision means the foresight that his art gave him, but *pro*vision implies the exercise of that foresight or *pre*vision; it is therefore better, because more comprehensive.

Mr. Collier's folio gives as an improvement upon Malone and Steeven's reading of the passage,—

> "And thy father
> Was Duke of Milan; and his only heir
> A princess; no worse issued,"—

the following:

> "And thy father
> Was Duke of Milan,—thou his only heir
> And princess no worse issued."

Supposing the reading of the folio to be ingenious rather than authoritative, the passage, as it stands in Hanmer, is decidedly better, because clearer:—

> "And thy father
> Was Duke of Milan,—thou, his only heir
> A princess—no worse issued."

In the next passage, given as emended by the folio, we have what appears to me one bad and one decidedly good alteration from the usual reading, which, in all the editions given hitherto, has left the meaning barely perceptible through the confusion and obscurity of the expression.

> "He being thus *lorded*,
> Not only with what my revenue yielded,
> But what my power might else exact,—like one
> Who having *unto truth* by telling of it
> Made such a sinner of his memory
> To credit his own lie,—he did believe
> He was indeed the Duke."

The folio says,—

> "He being thus *loaded*."

And to this change I object: the meaning was obvious before; "lorded" stands clearly enough here for made lord of, or, over, etc.; and though the expression is unusual, it is less prosaic than the proposed word *loaded*. But in the rest of the passage, the critic of the folio does immense service to the text, in reading

> " Like one
> Who having *to untruth* by telling of it
> Made such a sinner of his memory
> To credit his own lie,—he did believe
> He was indeed the Duke."

This change carries its own authority in its manifest good sense.

Of the passage,—

> " Whereon,
> A treacherous army levied, one midnight
> Fated to the purpose, did Antonio open
> The gates of Milan, and in the dead of darkness
> The ministers for the purpose hurried thence
> Me and thy crying self,"—

Mr. Collier says that the iteration of the word "purpose," in the fourth line, after its employment in the second, is a blemish, which his folio obviates by substituting the word *practice* in the first line. I think this a manifest improvement, though not an important one.

Mr. Collier gives Rowe the credit of having altered "butt" to *boat*, and "have quit it" to *had quit it*, in the lines—

> "Where they prepar'd
> A rotten carcase of a *butt* not rigg'd,
> Nor tackle, sail, nor mast—the very rats
> Instinctively *have quit it.*"

Adding, that in both changes he is supported by the corrector of the folio, 1632. Hanmer gives the passage exactly as the latter, and as Rowe does.

We now come to the stage-directions in the folio, to which Mr. Collier gives, I think, a most exaggerated value. He says, that, where Prospero says,—

> "Lend thy hand
> And pluck my magic garment from me,—so
> Lie there, my art,"—

the words "Lay it down," are written over against the passage. Now this really seems a very unnecessary direction, inasmuch as the next very clearly indicates that Prospero lays down as well as plucks off his "magic garment" —unless we are to suppose Miranda holding it over her arm till he resumes it. But still less do I agree with Mr. Collier in thinking the direction, "Put on robe again," at the passage beginning, "Now I arise," any extraordinary accession to the business, as it is technically called, of the scene; for I do not think that his resuming his magical robe was in any way necessary to account for the slumber which overcomes Miranda, "in spite of her interest in her father's story," and which Mr. Collier says the commentators have endeavoured to account for in various ways; but putting "*because* of her interest in her father's story," instead of "*in spite* of," I feel none of the difficulty which beset the commentators, and which Mr. Collier conjures by the stage-direction which makes Prospero resume his magic robe at a certain moment in order to put his daughter to sleep. Worthy Dr. Johnson, who was not among the puzzled commentators on this occasion, suggests, very agreeably to common sense, that

"Experience proves that any violent agitation of the mind easily subsides in slumber." But Mr. Collier says the Doctor gives this very reasonable explanation of Miranda's sleep only because he was not acquainted with the folio stage-direction about Prospero's coat, and knew no better. Now we are acquainted with this important addition to the text, and yet know no better than to agree with Dr. Johnson, that Miranda's slumbers were perfectly to be accounted for without the coat. Mr. Collier does not seem to know that a deeper and heavier desire to sleep follows upon the overstrained exercise of excited attention than on the weariness of a dull and uninteresting appeal to it.

But let us consider Shakespeare's text, rather than the corrector's additions, for a moment. Within reach of the wild wind and spray of the tempest, though sheltered from their fury, Miranda had watched the sinking ship struggling with the mad elements, and heard when "rose from sea to sky the wild farewell." Amazement and pity had thrown her into a paroxysm of grief, which is hardly allayed by her father's assurance, that "there's no harm done." After this terrible excitement follows the solemn exordium to her father's story :—

> "The hour's now come;
> The very minute bids thee ope thine ear
> Obey and be attentive."

The effort she calls upon her memory to make to recover the traces of her earliest impressions of life—the strangeness of the events unfolded to her—the duration of the recital itself, which is considerable—and, above all, the poignant personal interest of its details, are quite sufficient to account for the sudden utter prostration of her overstrained faculties and feelings, and the profound sleep that falls on the young girl. Perhaps Shakespeare knew this, though his commentators, old and new, seem not to have done so; and without a professed faith, such as some of us moderns indulge in, in the mysteries of magnetism, perhaps he believed enough in the magnetic force of the superior physical as well as mental power of Prospero's nature over the nervous, sensitive, irritable female organisation of his child to account for the "I know thou canst not choose" with which he concludes his observation on her drowsiness, and his desire that she will not resist it. The magic gown may, indeed, have been powerful; but hardly more so, I think, than the nervous exhaustion which, combined with the authoritative will and eyes of her lord and father, bowed down the child's drooping eyelids in profoundest sleep.

The strangest of all Mr. Collier's comments upon this passage, however, is that where he represents Miranda as, up to a certain point of her father's story, remaining "standing eagerly listening by his side." This is not only gratuitous, but absolutely contrary to Shakespeare's text—a greater authority, I presume, than even that of the annotated folio. Prospero's words to his daughter, when first he begins the recital of their sea-sorrow, are :—

> "Sit down!
> For thou must now know further."

Does Mr. Collier's folio reject this reading of the first line? Or does he suppose that Miranda remained standing, in spite of her father's command? Moreover, when he interrupts his story with the words, "Now I arise," he adds, to his daughter, "Sit still," which clearly indicates both that she was seated and that she was about to rise (naturally enough) when her father did. We say "Sit *down*" to a person who is standing; and "Sit *still*" to a person seated who is about to rise; and in all these minute particulars the simple text of Shakespeare, if attentively followed, gives every necessary indication of his intention with regard to the attitudes and movements of the persons on the stage in this scene; and the highly commended stage-directions of the folio are here, therefore, perfectly superfluous.

The next alteration in the received text is a decided improvement. In speaking of the royal fleet dispersed by the tempest, Ariel says:

> "They all have met again,
> And *are* upon the Mediterranean *flote*
> Bound sadly home for Naples;"—

for which Mr. Collier's folio substitutes:—

> "They all have met again,
> And all upon the Mediterranean *float*
> Bound sadly back to Naples."

Mr. Collier notices that the improvement of giving the lines,

> "Abhorred slave,
> Which any print of goodness will not take,"

to Prospero, instead of Miranda, dates as far back as Dryden and Davenant's alteration of "The Tempest," from which he says Theobald and others copied it.

The corrected folio gives its authority to the lines of the song:—

> "Foot it featly here and there,
> "And, sweet sprites, the burden bear,"—

which stands so in Hanmer, and, indeed, is the usually received arrangement of the song.

This is the last corrected passage in the first act, in the course of which Mr. Collier gives us no fewer than sixteen, altered, emended, and commented upon in his folio. Many of the emendations are to be found *verbatim* in the Oxford and subsequent editions, and three only appear to be of any special value, tried by the standard of common sense, to which it was agreed, on Mr. Collier's invitation, to refer them.

The line in Prospero's threat to Caliban :—

"I'll rack thee with old cramps,
Fill all thy bones with *aches*, make thee roar,"—

occasioned one of Mr. John Kemble's characteristic differences with the public, who objected, perhaps not without reason, to hearing the word "aches" pronounced as a dissyllable, although the line imperatively demands it; and Shakespeare shows that the word was not unusually so pronounced, as he introduces it with the same quantity in the prose dialogue of "Much Ado about Nothing," and makes it the vehicle of a pun which certainly argues that it was familiar to the public ear as *aches* and not *akes*. When Hero asks Beatrice, who complains that she is sick, what she is sick for,—a hawk, a hound, or a husband,—Beatrice replies, that she is sick for—or of—that which begins them all, an *ache*,—an *H*. Indeed, much later than Shakespeare's day the word was so pronounced; for Dean Swift, in the "City Shower," has the line,—

"Old *aches* throb, your hollow tooth will rage."

The opening of this play is connected with my earliest recollections. In looking down the "dark backward and abysm of time," to the period when I was but six years old, my memory conjures up a vision of a stately drawing-room on the ground-floor of a house, doubtless long since swept from the face of the earth by the encroaching tide of new houses and streets that has submerged every trace of suburban beauty, picturesqueness, or rural privacy in the neighbourhood of London, converting it all by a hideous process of assimilation into more London, till London seems almost more than England can carry.

But in those years, "long enough ago," to

which I refer,—somewhere between Lee and Blackheath, stood in the midst of well-kept grounds a goodly mansion, which held this pleasant room. It was always light and cheerful and warm, for the three windows down to the broad gravel-walk before it faced south; and though the lawn was darkened just in front of them by two magnificent yew-trees, the atmosphere of the room itself, in its silent, sunny loftiness, was at once gay and solemn to my small imagination and senses,—much as the interior of Saint Peter's of Rome has been since to them. Wonderful, large, tall jars of precious old china stood in each window, and my nose was just on a level with the wide necks, whence issued the mellowest smell of fragrant *pot-pourri*. Into this room, with its great crimson curtains and deep crimson carpet, in which my feet seemed to me buried, as in woodland moss, I used to be brought for the recompense of "having been very good," and there I used to find a lovely-looking lady, who was to me the fitting divinity of this shrine of pleasant awfulness. She bore a sweet Italian diminutive for her Christian name, added to one of the noblest old ducal names of Venice, which was that of her family.

I have since known that she was attached to the person of, and warmly personally attached to, the unfortunate Caroline of Brunswick, Princess of Wales,—then only unfortunate; so that I can now guess at the drift of much sad and passionate talk with indignant lips and tearful eyes, of which the meaning was then of course incomprehensible to me, but which I can now partly interpret by the subsequent history of that ill-used and ill-conducted lady.

The face of my friend with the great Venetian name was like one of Giorgione's pictures, —of that soft and mellow colourlessness that recalls the poet's line,—

"E smarrisce 'l bel volto in quel colore
Che non è pallidezza, ma candore,"—

or the Englishman's version of the same thought,

" Her face,—oh, call it fair, not pale!"

It seemed to me, as I remember it, cream-coloured; and her eyes, like clear water over brown rocks, where the sun is shining. But though the fair visage was like one of the great Venetian master's portraits, her voice was purely English, low, distinct, full, and soft,—and in this enchanting voice she used to tell me the story of the one large picture which adorned the room.

Over and over again, at my importunate beseeching, she told it,—sometimes standing before it, while I held her hand and listened with upturned face, and eyes rounding with big tears of wonder and pity, to a tale which shook my small soul with a sadness and strangeness far surpassing the interest of my beloved tragedy, "*The Babes in the Wood*," though at this period of my existence it has happened to me to interrupt with frantic cries of distress, and utterly refuse to hear, the end of that lamentable ballad.

But the picture.—In the midst of a stormy sea, on which night seemed fast settling down, a helmless, mastless, sailless bark lay weltering giddily, and in it sat a man in the full flower of vigorous manhood. His attitude was one of miserable dejection, and, oh, how I did long to remove the hand with which his eyes were covered, to see what manner of look in them answered to the bitter sorrow which the speechless lips expressed! His other hand rested on the fair curls of a girl-baby of three years old, who clung to his knee, and, with wide, wondering blue eyes and laughing lips, looked up into the half-hidden face of her father.—"And that," said the sweet voice at my side, "was the good Duke of Milan, Prospero,—and that was his little child, Miranda."

There was something about the face and figure of the Prospero that suggested to me those of my father; and this, perhaps, added to the poignancy with which the representation of his distress affected my childish imagination. But the impression made by the picture, the story, and the place where I heard the one and saw the other, is among the most vivid that my memory retains. And never, even now, do I turn the magic page that holds that marvellous history, without again seeing the lovely lady, the picture full of sad dismay, and my own six-year-old self listening to that earliest Shakespearian lore that my mind and heart ever received. I suppose this is partly the secret of my love for this, above all other of the poet's plays:—it was my first possession in the kingdom of unbounded delight which he has since bestowed upon me.

NOTES ON THE TEMPEST.

No. II.

NOTES ON THE TEMPEST.

No. II.

THE *Tempest* is, as I have already said, my favourite of Shakespeare's Dramas. The remoteness of the scene from all known localities allows a range to the imagination such as no other of his plays affords—not even the *Midsummer Night's Dream*, where, though the *dramatis personæ* are half of them superhuman, the scene is laid in a wood "near Athens;" and Theseus and Hypolita, if fabulous folk, are among the mythological acquaintance of our earliest school days.

But the "uninhabited Island," lost in unknown seas, gives far other scope to the wandering fancy. As the scene is removed from all places with which we hold acquaintance, so the story, simple in the extreme, has more reference to past events than to any action in the play itself, which involves but few incidents, and has little to do with common experience.

But chiefly I delight in this play, because of the image which it presents to my mind of the glorious supremacy of the righteous human soul over all things by which it is surrounded. Prospero is to me the representative of wise and virtuous manhood, in its true relation to the combined elements of existence—the physical powers of the external world, and the varieties of character with which it comes into voluntary, accidental, or enforced contact.

Of the wonderful chain of being, of which Caliban is the densest and Ariel the most ethereal extreme, Prospero is the middle link. He—the wise and good man—is the ruling power, to whom the whole series is subject.

First, and lowest in the scale, comes the gross and uncouth but powerful savage, who represents both the more ponderous and unwieldy natural elements (as the earth and water), which the wise Magician by his knowledge compels to his service; and the brutal and animal propensities of the nature of man, which he, the type of its noblest development, holds in lordly subjugation.

Next follow the drunken, ribald, foolish retainers of the King of Naples, whose ignorance, knavery, and stupidity represent the coarser attributes of those great unenlightened masses, which in all communities threaten authority by their conjunction with brute force and savage· ferocity; and only under the wholesome restraint of a wise discipline can be gradually admonished into the salutary subserviency necessary for their civilisation.

Ascending by degrees in the scale, the next group is that of the cunning, cruel, selfish, treacherous worldlings—Princes and Potentates —the peers in outward circumstances of high birth and breeding of the noble Prospero— whose villanous policy (not unaided by his own dereliction of his duties as a governor in the pursuit of his pleasure as a philosopher) triumphs over his fortune, and, through a devilish ability and craft, for a time gets the better of truth and virtue in his person.

From these, who represent the baser intellectual as the former do the baser sensual properties of humanity, we approach by a most harmonious moral transition, through the agency of the skilfully interposed figure of the kindly gentleman, Gonzalo, those charming types of youth and love, Ferdinand and Miranda—the fervent chivalrous devotion of the youth, and the yielding simplicity and sweetness of the girl, are lovely representations of those natural emotions of tender sentiment and passionate desire which, watched and guided and guarded by the affectionate solicitude and paternal prudence of Prospero, are pruned of their lavish luxuriance and supported in their violent weakness by the wise will that teaches forbearance and self-control as the only price at which these exquisite flowers of existence may unfold their blossoms in prosperous beauty, and bear their rightful harvest of happiness as well as pleasure.

Next in this wonderful gamut of being, governed by the sovereign soul of Prospero, come the shining figures of the Masque— beautiful bright apparitions, fitly indicating the air, the fire, and all the more smiling aspects and subtler forces of nature. These minister with prompt obedience to the magical behests of Science, and, when not toiling in appointed service for their great task-master, recreate and refresh his senses and his spirit with the every-varying pageant of this beautiful Universe.

Last—highest of all—crowning with a fitful flame of lambent brightness this poetical pyramid of existence, flickers and flashes the beautiful Demon, without whose exquisite companionship we never think of the royal Magician with his grave countenance of command—Ariel seems to me to represent the keenest perceiving intellect—apart from all moral consciousness and sense of responsibility. His power and knowledge are in some respects greater than those of his master—he can do what Prospero cannot—he lashes up the Tempest round the Island—he saves the King and his companions from the shipwreck—he defeats the conspiracy of Sebastian and Antonio, and discovers the clumsy plot of the beast Caliban—he wields immediate influence over the elements, and comprehends alike without indignation or sympathy—which are moral results—the sin and suffering of humanity. Therefore, because he is only a spirit of knowledge, he is subject to the spirit of love—and the wild, subtle, keen, beautiful, powerful creature is compelled to serve with mutinous waywardness and unwilling subjection the human soul that pitied and rescued it from its harsher slavery to sin—and which, though controlling it with a wise severity to the fulfilment of its duties, yearns after it with the tearful eyes of tender human love when its wild wings flash away into its newly-recovered realm of lawless liberty.

NOTES ON THE TEMPEST.

No. III.

NOTES ON THE TEMPEST.

No. III.

IN the second act we have the passage relating to the Princess Claribel's marriage to the King of Tunis,—

> "And the fair soul herself
> Weigh'd between lothness and obedience at
> Which end o' the beam *should* bow."

Malone considers that the *should* of the old copy was merely an elliptical *she would*, and gives the lines thus,—

> "Weigh'd between lothness and obedience at
> Which end of the beam *she'd* bow;"—

a version which has been most generally adopted by subsequent editors. Mr. Collier, however, proposes as an improvement on this, the alteration which he finds in his folio, and gives the passage thus :—

> "And the fair soul herself,
> Weigh'd between lothness and obedience, *as*
> Which end of the beam should bow;"—

which I cannot think at all less "detrimental to the sense" than he finds Malone's correction. In Hanmer we have what appears to me a much better reading of the passage, by the mere omission of the preposition "of" in the third line :—

> "And the fair soul herself
> Weigh'd between lothness and obedience at
> Which end the beam should bow."

This appears to me the best version of the lines given yet; and Pope thought so too, for he adopted it.

The next emendation to which I object is in the speech of Antonio, beginning, "She that is Queen of Tunis," the passage which in the old folio is printed thus :—

> "*She that from whom*
> We were sea-swallow'd,"—

was emended by Rowe by omitting "that" and printing "She from whom;" and this reading has been universally adopted since. It seems curious to me that no one bethought themselves of transposing "She that" into "That she," which would have been Shakespearian, and justified the retention of the otherwise incomprehensible *that*. However, Mr. Collier's folio omits "that," and alters another member of the passage, substituting the word *for* instead of *from*:—

"She *for* whom
We were all sea-swallow'd,"—

a change which he pronounces an improvement. I scarcely think it so: "from whom" clearly indicates the meaning of "coming from whom;" at any rate, the change is quite unimportant.

The next emendation in the passage which Mr. Collier finds in his folio he rejects, saying the original reading seems preferable, and this is,—

"How shall that Claribel
Measure *us* back to Naples,"

which Mr. Collier's folio changes into "measure *it* back to Naples;" and strangely enough the Oxford edition has that same alteration in the text; but inasmuch as the whole passage stands thus :—

> "A space whose every cubit
> Seems to cry out, 'How shall that Claribel
> Measure us back to Naples?'"

and that the many cubits which intervene between Tunis and Naples are supposed to utter the observation, "Measure *us* back" is obviously the more appropriate reading of the line.

The next change in the text which Mr. Collier produces seems again unimportant. He says Alonzo's exclamation on waking and finding Sebastian and Antonio with their swords drawn has always been given,—

> "Why are you drawn?
> Wherefore *this* ghastly looking?"

and that upon the showing of his copy, the *this* is a misprint for *thus*,—

> "Wherefore thus ghastly looking?"

He says the change is not absolutely necessary. I should say it was absolutely unnecessary.

The crossing of the T in Gonzalo's assertion that "there was a noise that's verity" (the old copy reads *verily*), a merit which Mr. Collier imputes to his corrector, is to be found in Hanmer—Pope being the originator of the correction, which, though consisting merely of the alteration of a letter, materially affects the sense.

In the soliloquy of Trinculo, which ends by his hiding under Caliban's gabardine, Mr. Collier's folio says that the words, "I will here shroud till the *dregs* of the storm be past," should be, "I will here shroud till the *drench of the* storm be past," which he justifies upon the ground that Trinculo would perhaps have thought it more desirable to avoid the drench or extreme violence of the storm than the mere dregs or conclusion of it. But the dregs of anything are its thickest and heaviest part—the sediment, the dirty residuum, deposited by liquid—and therefore, upon the whole, the least desirable part of the storm, even though it be its conclusion—especially, as according to Trinculo's apprehensive description of the threatening sky, one cloud was hovering in it which he compares to a "foul bumbard" (a barrel for holding liquor), the lees or "dregs" of which are assuredly not the pleasantest part to receive upon one's head. This emendation I therefore do not accept as such.

The next alteration of the text given is the omission of the syllable "ing" from the word trencher in Caliban's song:—

"Nor scrape trencher*ing*, nor wash dish."

Theobald and Dryden both wrote the passage as Mr. Collier's folio has it, "nor scrape trencher." Many of the subsequent editors, however, retain "trenchering," which may perhaps be considered as a term for trenchers collectively, Caliban meaning by the trenchering of the table all the trenchers used upon it. The omission is a decided improvement, I think, and is to be found also in Hanmer.

The opening lines of the third act, spoken by Ferdinand while employed in log-bearing for the love of Miranda, conclude with a passage about which there has been much discussion :—

> "But these sweet thoughts do e'en refresh my labours
> Most busy lest when I do it."

This is the version given by the earliest folio of 1623; in the folio of 1632 again the passage stands,—

> "Most busy least when I do it,"

which Mr. Collier says is the usual reading of the passage. But Mr. Theobald's suggestion of reading it "Most busy less" (*i.e.* least oppressed or absorbed with business) has been adopted by almost all subsequent editors. Of this decided improvement on the original text Mr. Collier takes no notice, though it involves but the change of one letter, but strongly commends the reading given in his corrected folio, of—

> "Most busy—blest when I do it,"

which he says is undoubtedly the right reading

of the passage corrupted by the accidental omission of the letter *b* for two centuries and a half. I cannot at all agree that this alteration is superior to Theobald's; the sense is more obscure, and the line is rendered harsh and ungraceful by the abrupt break in it; whereas in Theobald's version the line is smooth to the tongue, and quite as intelligible to the comprehension: while Sir Thomas Hanmer gives a far bolder departure from the text, and not satisfied with changing one letter, alters the word *most* into its direct opposite, *least*—

"Least busy when I do it;"

upon what authority, I know not. The passage of course has the same meaning as Theobald's, but has not the merit of his near conformity to the text of the earliest folio.

The next emendation is in Prospero's speech to Ferdinand, when he bestows Miranda upon him,—

"For I
Have given you a third of mine own life,"

which Mr. Collier's corrected folio reads a

"*thread* of my own life," and all the modern editors so write the passage. Mr. Collier, however, does not seem to accept the explanation which some commentators have been satisfied with, that "third" in the old folio is simply an obsolete way of spelling thread, of which Hawkins and Steevens both give examples.

The exquisite lines addressed by Isis to Ceres in the Masque have afforded infinite scope to the various editors of Shakespeare, after whose lucubrations on them nothing more restorative can be imagined than to read the passage itself, redolent as it is with all the freshest fragrance of earth, air, and water.

"Thy banks with pionied and twilled brims,"

reads the original folio, which Mr. Collier's emended copy corrects into "pioned and tilled brims," pioned meaning, according to him (and he can show Spencer for authority), dug, or turned with a spade; the French words *pioche*, and *piocher*, a rough spade, and to dig roughly, are kindred to "pioned;" but besides that the use of that word was certainly uncommon even in Shakespeare's time, the passage becomes tautological, as well as rather prosaically agricultural, by this admission of a second word, "tilled," having so nearly the meaning of the first. Shakespeare is not apt to be so poor in resources; some commentators insist that twilled means twill pants, some species of flower, of which we have lost either the kind, or this denomination; others convert the line into "peonied and lilied," giving many learned references to the chaste virtues supposed to reside in peonies and lilies; and Sir Thomas Hanmer, having perhaps some theory of his own to warrant the introduction of the gaudiest of Flora's darlings, writes the line—

"With peonied and tulip'd brims,"—

a very violent emendation of the text, to say nothing of the discord produced to the eye of the imagination by the scarlet and yellow flames of this oriental flower blazing among the soft elements of rural English beauty, which fill the preceding lines, and amid which, tulips seem as little appropriate as they are to make "cold nymphs chaste crowns."

But to return to Mr. Collier's proposed emendation of "pioned and tilled," his folio version was given by Mr. Holt merely as a conjecture, and Steevens gives the line so corrected to him in one of his notes. Upon the whole, the pleasantest, and therefore the best emendation of the line, when all are equally uncertain, seems that which matches best with the tone and colouring of the rest of the picture, and the peonied and lilied banks betrimmed by spongy April, are better in this respect than anything else offered to Shakespeare's readers by the painful industry of his commentators.

Of the blessing pronounced upon Ferdinand and Miranda, all the lines were originally attributed to Juno. Theobald, with nice poetical discrimination, gives the latter portion of them to Ceres, a change in which Sir Thomas Hanmer and all subsequent editors coincide. Mr. Collier's folio, however, adheres to the original text in this particular; and the general character of these emendations perhaps accounts sufficiently for this not being found among them, suggested as it is, more by poetical feeling than critical acumen: whoever the unknown commentator was, he was assuredly not a poet. Farther on, the folio alters the lines—

> "Spring come to you at the farthest
> In the very end of harvest,"

to "*Rain* come to you at the farthest," a change which Mr. Collier pronounces "important," but which seems to me anything but an improvement. It is very true, that rain before the "very end of harvest" would be unwelcome, but in that sense the line ought to be—" Rain come to you at the *earliest*"—not at the *farthest;* *i.e.* may your very first rain not fall till the harvest is carried. But I think the passage simply means that spring shall rapidly succeed autumn, leaving the dreary winter out of the calendar, a blessing Shakespeare has borrowed from that proclaimed to the Jews in that wonderful and awful chapter of promises and threats, the 26th of Leviticus, "And your threshing shall reach unto the vintage, and the vintage shall reach unto the sowing time."

From the same chapter he takes the words, "Earth's increase." While observing upon these biblical expressions, of which Caliban's picturesque

> "And taught me how
> To name the bigger light, and how the less,
> That burn by day and night"

is one borrowed from Genesis, it cannot but seem to every thoughtful reader of Shakespeare how absolutely pervaded his language is with the spirit and form of that most precious treasure of our tongue, the English Bible. It has been a question how much of Greek—if any—how much of Latin, and the modern French and Italian languages, our great dramatist possessed; and little proof can be found of his having anything but the most superficial acquaintance with any language but his own;

but it is impossible to read his plays attentively without perceiving that his mind was absolutely imbued with the style of thought and expression of our Bible. And strange to say, an intimate familiarity with the peculiar characteristics of its language is infinitely more perceptible in his profane (not to use the word in any but its technical sense) plays, than in the great sacred epic of our English tongue, the *Paradise Lost*, whose learned author had assuredly the Bible in his heart, but so great a store of Greek, Latin, and Italian lore in his head, that though the subject of his poem is purely biblical, the style seldom, if ever, recalls that of the Bible; while in reading his noble Jewish tragedy of the Samson, the Greek dramatists occur to us half a dozen times for once that we are reminded of the wild story of the Israelitish hero and his Philistian persecutors as it stands in the book of Judges.

And well it is for us and for him that our profane playwright knew his Bible as he did;— that book, of which one of the most eminent seceders from the Church of England—John Henry Newman—said, that it was the most formidable obstacle that Roman Catholic propagandists have to encounter in converting English Protestants;—their Bible, of which the pure and noble language becomes betimes so familiar to their minds and mouths, that it is impossible to present to them the truth clothed in any words which can approach in lucid sublimity those that lie, God be thanked! on every cottage chimney throughout the English land.

The copious inspiration Shakespeare drew from this source has made his plays the lay Bible of Englishmen; and it is curious enough that the ignorant among them misquote him for Holy Writ sometimes (but never Milton), seduced, like the worthy Judge in Texas, by the similitude of speech and spirit, into substituting the words of poetical for those of sacred inspiration.

The change of the word "wise" for "wife" in the lines

> "So rare a wondered father and a *wise*,
> Makes this place Paradise,"

receives the sanction of Mr. Collier's folio. The passage is so printed by Hanmer, Malone and the later editors all concur in the change, so that the authority of the folio corrector seems hardly needed to recommend it.

In the folio's next emendation, namely, that of *winding* instead of *windring* brooks in the speech of Iris, the Oxford edition again has the identical correction proposed by Mr. Collier's authority, and Steevens says that all the modern editors read winding for windring, but himself proposes the word wand'ring, which I prefer, for, like winding, it does but change one letter of the original text, but at the same time gives the line a fuller and more musical sound, by the substitution of the vowel *a* for the vowel *i* in the word—a consideration by no means to be overlooked in verse, which is musical speech,—and dramatic verse, which is written expressly to be spoken; of course "other things being equal."

In going through the second and third acts of the *Tempest* with Mr. Collier's volume of corrections, I find five only out of sixteen which appear to me of any peculiar value tested by common sense; the rest I think are either indifferent or objectionable, and of the five which are decided improvements, every one is found in Hanmer and other of the early editors.

Before closing my observations on the second and third Acts of the *Tempest*, I would suggest to the reader's consideration the curious felicity of the scene when Ferdinand and Miranda acknowledge their affection to each other. I mean in the harmonious contrast between a young prince, bred in a Court, himself the centre of a sphere of the most artificial civilisation, and a girl not only without any knowledge of the world and society, but even without previous knowledge of the existence of any created man but her father and Caliban.

Brought up in all but utter solitude, under no influence but that of her wise and loving father on earth, and her wise and loving Father in Heaven, Miranda exhibits no more coyness in her acceptance of Ferdinand's overtures than properly belongs to the instinctive modesty of her sex, unenhanced by any of the petty pretty arts of coquetry and assumed shyness, which are the express result of artificial female training. The simple emotion of bashfulness, indeed, which (in spite of her half-astonished, half-delighted exclamation—

"Do you love me?"

that elicits her lover's passionate declaration) causes her to "weep at what she's glad of," is so little comprehensible to herself, that she shakes it off with something like self-reproach, as an involuntary disingenuousness: "Hence, bashful *cunning;*" and then with that most pathetic and exquisite invocation to "plain and holy innocence" offers her life to her lover with the perfect devotion and humility of the true womanly nature:—

"To be your fellow
You may deny me, but I'll be your servant
Whether you will or no."

In the purity and simplicity of this "tender of affection," Ferdinand made acquaintance with a species of modesty to which assuredly none of those ladies of the Court of Naples, "whom he had eyed with best regard," had ever introduced him; and indeed to them Miranda's proceeding might very probably have appeared highly unlady-like, as I have heard it pronounced more than once by—ladies. The young prince, however, was probably himself surprised for a little while into a sphere of earnest sincerity, as different from the artificial gallantry with which he had encountered the former objects of his admiration as the severe manual labour he was undergoing for the sake of Miranda was different from the inflated offers of service, and professions of slavery, which were the jargon of civilised courtesy;—that species of language which Olivia reproves when she says

"'Twas never merry world
Since lowly feigning was called compliment."

The transparent simplicity and sweet solemnity of the girl's confession of love could not but awaken an almost religious sense of honour and tenderness in the young man's soul, and though his Neapolitan Court vocabulary speaks a little in the

> "Admired Miranda
> Indeed the top of admiration,"

the

> "I
> Beyond all limit of what else i' the world
> Do love, prize, honour you,"

is love's true utterance, as free from sophistication as the girl's own guileless challenge.

It is not a little edifying to reflect how different Prospero's treatment of these young people's case would have been, if, instead of only the most extraordinary of conjurors, he had been the most commonplace of scheming matrons of the present day. He, poor man, alarmed at the sudden conquest Ferdinand makes of his child, and perceiving that he must "this swift business uneasy make, lest two light winning make the prize light," can bethink himself of no better expedient than reducing the poor young prince into a sort of supplementary Caliban, a hewer of wood and drawer of water:—now, a modern chaperon would merely have had to intimate to a well-trained modern young lady, that it would be as well not to give the young gentleman too much encouragement, till his pretensions to the throne of Naples could really be made out (his straying about without any Duke of Newcastle, and very wet, was a good deal like a mere adventurer, you know); and I am pretty certain that the judicious mamma or female guardian of Miss Penelope Smith, the fair British Islander who became Princess of Capua, pursued no other system of provocation by repression. An expert matrimonial schemer of the present day, I say, would have devised by these means a species of trial by torture for poor Ferdinand, to which his "sweating labour" in Prospero's patient log man would have been luxurious idleness.

But Prospero was after all a mere man, and knew no better than to bring up Miranda to speak the truth, and the fair child had been so holily trained by him, that her surrender of herself to the man she loves is so little feminine after the approved feminine fashion, that it is simply angelic.

That Shakespeare, who indeed knew all things, knew very well the difference between such a creature as Miranda and a well-brought-up young lady, is plain enough, when he makes poor Juliet, after her passionate confession of love made to the stars, and overheard by Romeo, apologise to him with quite pathetic mortification for not having been more "strange." She regrets extremely her unqualified expressions of affection,—assures Romeo that nothing would have induced her to have spoken the truth, if she had only known he heard her, and even offers, if it can be the least satisfaction to him, and redeem what she may have lost in his esteem by her frankness, to "frown and be perverse and say him nay,"—and in short has evidently shocked her own conventional prejudices quite as much as she fears she has his, by not having had a chance of playing a thousand fantastical tricks about a passion which is thenceforth to govern her life, and give her over to her early death. But then Juliet was the flower of Veronese young ladies, and her good mother, and gossiping nurse, were not likely to have neglected her education to the tune of letting her speak the truth without due preparation. Miranda is to be excused as a savage—probably Ferdinand thought her excusable.

To any one desirous of enhancing by comparison their appreciation of the *Tempest*, I would recommend, not the perusal of, but a glance into, Dryden and D'Avenant's alteration of it, "The Enchanted Island." This gross burlesque, perpetrated by a man of singular genius, who had indeed "fallen on evil days," and ventured to lay unhallowed hands on Shakespeare's work, is the finest comment by contrast that could be devised upon his divine poem. It was my misfortune, many years ago, to see this coarse and ludicrous parody represented on the English stage, whence it is to be hoped the better taste of later days has banished it for ever.

NOTES ON
ROMEO AND JULIET.

NOTES ON

ROMEO AND JULIET.[1]

ROMEO represents the *sentiment*, and Juliet the *passion* of love.

The *pathos* is his, the *power* hers.

His first scene is mere rose-light before sun-rising; the key-note to the after *real* love and life is given in the lines,—

"I fear too early," etc.

The spirit of the balcony scene is that of joyful tenderness, and something of a sort of sweet

---

[1] [These few notes were addressed as mere suggestions to a gentleman studying the part of Romeo, who did me the honour to consult me upon his rendering of the part. They are neither an analysis of the play nor of the character, but mere *hints for acting*.—F. A. K.]

surprise at the fervid girl-passion which suddenly wraps him round, and carries him as with wings of fire towards the level of its own intensity.

All the succeeding scenes are pervaded by the elastic spirit of joy and triumph of his secret happiness. Mercutio's death is the sudden heavy thunder-cloud in the bright sky; his own duel with Tybalt—the breaking of the lightning storm, and the falling of the bolt that strikes and shatters his green tree of life. His furious burst of uncontrolled rage and hatred is followed by the utter collapse of all passion, leaving only *consciousness*, but no *discrimination* of infinite trouble—a nightmare of indefinite abysmal misery.

The scene in the friar's cell is the sheer expression of the *violence of weakness*—haggard bewilderment. Hunted for his life by the Capulets, hidden from the pursuit of justice, *palpitating with nervous anguish*, apprehensive of instantaneous revengeful murder, expectant of inevitable sentence of death, overwhelmed with horror of his own sanguinary deed, because his victim is kinsman to his wife, filled with passionate longing and desire for the possession of that wife, for which all preparation had been made, even for that night, the spirit of the whole scene, from its beginning to its end, is summed up in the speech, beginning

"Thou canst not speak of what thou dost not feel."

Gradually, as the friar utters his concluding admonition, the vital invincible hope of youth, and the anticipation of the "joy past joy," which beckon him, rise triumphant above all the misery and culminate in the farewell.

In the parting scene in Juliet's room, she languid with passion, wan with woe, beneath his reiterated tender offering of his life to her, the throbbing of the natural desire to live,—here again his self-sacrifice is the sentiment, her selfishness the passion of love.

The opening of the fifth act is a gentle, tender, melancholy ecstasy, a blending of exquisite memories and hopes in a pervading atmosphere of sadness.

After the news of Juliet's death, one *blasphemous* outburst of mad agony follows, and then the iron gloom of utter despair, the blackness of darkness, the absolute *possession* by misery of his whole being, *through which* his dwelling on the details of the apothecary's existence, his one or two sobs of tenderness:—

"Hast thou no letters to me from the friar?
Well, Juliet, I will lie with thee to-night."

his farewell to Balthasar, his warning to Paris, his recognition of him after killing him,—all are lingering and broken touches of the sweet, tender, pathetic nature, choked with the bitterness of his fate, and breaking through the settled, sullen, savage hardness of his despair.

I am not careless, as I may have appeared to you, of the value of the text of Shakespeare; but, poet, philosopher, and playwright as he was, your dealings with him are in the latter capacity only. You need not be afraid of eliminating the two nobler elements of his works; omit what you will, that is *impossible*.

Remember too, that his *inspiration*—and I use the word advisedly—did not protect him from the errors of his time and place. As for occasional breaking of his lines, my excitement the other evening made them more frequent than they really were; and a good musician should know how to redeem a faulty line, in some measure, by his utterance.

www.ingramcontent.com/pod-product-compliance
Lightning Source LLC
Chambersburg PA
CBHW020306170426
43202CB00008B/518